WALKING BEANS WASN'T SOMETHING YOU DID WITH YOUR DOG

*Stories of Growing up in and
Around Small Towns in the Midwest*

Edited by Jean Tennant

Published by: Shapato Publishing
PO Box 476
Everly, IA 51338

ISBN: 978-0-9821058-0-1

Library of Congress Control Number: 2008908228
First Printing September 2008

This book is dedicated to my family: My children, Shaun Iske, Paul Iske and Toni Simon, for lending their names to the creation of Shapato Publishing, and to my husband, Grover Reiser, for his encouragement, patience, and sense of humor while I completed this project.

Jean Tennant

More praise for *Walking Beans Wasn't Something You Did With Your Dog*:

A fascinating, insightful and fun romp through the fields of memory. As the writers unfold their various stories, you'll wish you'd been there.
~Mark Leslie, author of *One Hand Screaming*
www.MarkLeslie.ca

Walking Beans will walk into your heart. A treasure chest of touching and fun stories, it definitely offers continuity to the values and fun experienced by my grandparents, parents, and my generation of twentysomethings. Like a good Midwestern buffet, *Walking Beans* will please appetites of the entire family.
~Stacie Ruth Stoelting
CBN.com Columnist, Author of *Still Holding Hands*, Recording Artist and founder of Bright Light Ministry.
www.brightlightministry.com

Walking Beans is a delightful compilation of stories that will delight your soul. It's a great read.
~Joan R. Burney, Author, Columnist, Counselor.

Acknowledgments

A book like this isn't possible without the cooperation of many people. First and foremost, I need to thank the Arts on Grand Writers' Group of Spencer, Iowa, for providing many of the stories presented here. Their stories, which they generously shared with me over the years, first sparked my interest and had me asking for more. That created the germ of an idea, which in turn led to the compilation of this book. I won't attempt to name them all, as members tend to come and go, but they know who they are and how much I appreciate their help.

I also must thank my friend, Betty Taylor, for her tireless editing, feedback and general advice. She went far above and beyond the call of duty, even to using her husband as a captive audience and sounding board during long car trips.

Thank you to Terri Branson, owner and publisher of Dragonfly Publishing, for her generosity of spirit, not to mention her quick and detailed answers to my many questions.

Thank you to Paula Berinstein, host of The Writing Show podcast, who's been a long-distance friend and an inspiration.

Thank you, also, to my proofreaders. They worked tirelessly and often on short notice. Any remaining errors in this book—and I've been assured *something* will get through—are entirely my own fault.

This book has truly been a labor of love. I hope you enjoy reading it as much as I've enjoyed the process of putting it together.

Jean Tennant
Shapato Publishing
Everly, Iowa

CONTENTS

WALKING BEANS WASN'T SOMETHING YOU DID WITH YOUR DOG

*Stories of Growing up in and
Around Small Towns in the Midwest*

Edited by Jean Tennant

Drawing by LaVonne Hansen. Blue Ribbon winner, Clay County Fair 2002

LaVonne Hansen lives in Hartley, Iowa. She's an artist who presents "chalk talks" in Iowa, Arizona and Canada. Some of her award-winning, pen-and-ink drawings appear in these pages.

HOW OUR DOG GOT HIS NEW NAME

Dannie Weir Larsen

Randy was a Border Collie mix, four years old the summer he got a new name. Black and white, with a black patch over one eye, he was born in our barn to Angel, his mother, and a father of unknown origin. Randy, the smallest of the litter, was the only one we kept, and he was my pal.

We lived on a farm in a small town in Southern Iowa, and as a farmer's daughter I spent a fair portion of my summer months helping with chores. By the time I was eight I was well versed in how to gather eggs, as well as feed the chickens and other small livestock. We had cattle and sometimes a hog or two on our 60-acre farm, but my brothers Arlen and Chris had the task of caring for them. As the only girl, and the baby of the family, I was cut some slack. But not much.

For at least one full month during the summer I would spend several hours each day "walking beans." Walking beans back then wasn't the easy job it would later become. When my brothers and I walked beans, we literally walked through the rows of soybeans, bending low to pull the weeds from the earth with our gloved hands. After a couple of hours of this our backs felt like they were ready to snap in half, our shoulders ached and our arms seemed to weigh fifty pounds each. Randy often kept us company on these long, hot days, and his antics were the only bright spot to an otherwise tedious and difficult task.

"You missed one," my brother Chris would call out from his place several rows to one side of me.

"Take care of your own rows," I'd snap back, too tired to care that he could, if provoked, lob a dirt ball at me with deadly accuracy.

Then, when I was twelve, a family moved into the empty farmhouse a half mile from ours, on the same section. I was thrilled to learn the family had a girl my own age and that she would, in fact, be going to my school in the fall. So when she made her way over to our place early one morning, I hurried outside to greet her.

"My name's Alice," she told me. She stood next to our family pickup, a dented old Ford, in her tidy slacks with a crease down the front and a sleeveless top that was equally spotless. I felt frumpy in my bibs and an oversized T-shirt that had once been my brother's. But I was so happy to have another girl within playing distance that I was willing to overlook her flaws. I'd heard that the new family was from some big city in Florida, and no doubt she hadn't yet figured out how to fit in.

"Do you want to come over to my place?" she asked. "My dad built a tree house for me."

A tree house! My brothers had a tree house, but they never let me in it.

"Sure—" I started to say, then stopped. I couldn't just run off to play, no matter how much I wanted to. I had chores to do. "I can't. I have to walk beans today. Maybe I could come over later? When I'm done?" I finished hopefully.

Her expression showed puzzlement. Then Randy strolled over, tail wagging, to see what we were up to and if anyone possibly had a treat for him. Alice's eyes traveled to Randy. "Is that him?" she asked. Before I understood what she was talking about, she bent and held her hand out to our dog. "Hiya, Beans. C'mere, Beans."

At that moment my brother Chris barreled out of the house, just in time to hear this exchange. Chris howled with laughter.

"No, that's not—" I started, but before I could finish, Randy, ears perked as though he'd been called by an old friend, trotted over to Alice and eagerly placed his head beneath her outstretched hand.

Alice scratched our dog's ears. "Nice boy, Beans," she cooed, and Randy responded by jumping up and muddying the front of her clean top with his paws. She didn't seem to mind. But she did look over at Chris, nearly rolling around in the dirt at this point, as though wondering what had gotten into him. Then Arlen came out of the house to see what all the commotion was about, and Chris filled him in. By now Alice understood she'd made an error, and she blushed as bright a pink as her pretty blouse. Arlen, the more diplomatic-minded of my brothers, choked back his laughter to explain to Alice: "Our dog's name is Randy."

Alice looked over at me. "But you said you had to walk Beans today."

Chris howled anew. Arlen patiently told our new neighbor, "Walking beans means we have to go out into the soybean fields and pull up weeds all day."

"Oh," Alice said in a very small voice. I could see she was embarrassed, and I was furious with Chris for making her feel worse. And Randy certainly hadn't helped matters by going to her when she'd called him by the wrong name.

I told Alice I could play later, if she still wanted to, and I *was* eager to see that tree house. She shrugged and said sure, but I couldn't help but wonder if we'd scared her off. Surely she thought we were a family of lunatics.

After Alice was gone, Arlen and I went to the pickup. I hopped in the front seat and Arlen got in behind the steering wheel. Though he was only fourteen, he would drive us to the other end of the soybean field, where we'd begin our day's work. I was secretly hoping Arlen would leave Chris behind—who needed him?—but, as he turned the key in the ignition and started the engine, he stuck his head out the window and yelled, "Hurry up, will ya? Or are you going to lay around in the dirt all day?"

Chris, still reeling with hilarity, picked himself up off the ground and trotted to the pickup. Then, to my dismay, he called to Randy, "C'mon, Beans, get in."

And Randy, happy to be invited, leapt into the bed of the pickup as Chris squeezed in the front seat next to me.

"Don't call him that!" I hollered at Chris. "He'll think it's really his name."

"He already thinks that," Chris smirked. "Don't ya, Beans?" he yelled over his shoulder.

"You're making it worse." I punched Chris on the arm. He shoved me back, not too hard.

As we walked the bean field that day, Randy kept pace, occasionally veering off to explore. Chris, probably to irritate me more than anything, continued to call our dog Beans.

"Hey, Beans, I see a rabbit. Better get it!" he yelled as Randy walked alongside me in my row.

"Stop it!" I wailed, but Randy obligingly streaked off in pursuit of a rabbit he would never catch.

For the rest of the day I tried to ignore my brothers and concentrate on the tedious task of pulling up weeds. When Arlen also started calling our dog Beans, I fumed. At the supper table that night, I complained to our parents how my rotten, stupid brothers kept calling our dog Beans. Unfortunately, when Arlen explained the circumstances, our parents also thought it was hilarious, and by the end of the day our dog had a new name.

Stubborn to the core, I attempted to hold off for a few more days, but finally even I admitted defeat and started calling our dog Beans. My eventual capitulation may have come about in part because Alice and I became good friends. I went to her house often that summer—usually accompanied by Beans—and we'd play in her tree house, which was every bit as impressive as she'd described.

Alice even forgave my brothers for embarrassing her that first day. She had to, because after that rather rocky start, Alice was to become not only my best friend, but my sister-in-law as well.

Dannie Weir Larsen grew up on a farm in Missouri. She's a homemaker, now living in Chicago.

WALKING BEANS WASN'T SOMETHING YOU DID WITH YOUR DOG

CYRANO THE PIG

Marshall Anderson

Maybe at first glance a story about a pig doesn't hold much appeal, but Cyrano was a very special pig.

I was about nine years old in the summer of 1955, and lived on a farm in rural Nebraska under the generally liberal guidance of my mom and dad. I was the tail-ender by quite a margin, of four brothers who had already flown the nest. So my folks, who had largely tired of the discipline thing, left me much to my own devices except at chore time, when I was expected to pull my own weight. We milked by hand five cows—Millie, Star, Polly, Mavis and Geranium, who was mine. My dad had given her to me when she was a baby. I'd raised her on a bottle, and gave her much petting and affection as she grew up into a fine Holstein who rewarded me with an occasional slobbery lick as well as an occasional swat of her tail, and had a habit of standing on a few of my barefoot toes if I wasn't careful.

That spring Uncle Hjalmar—that's the mangled Scandinavian spelling of the name Elmer—thought I should also have a pig, so he gave me a baby pig about half the size of a cat. I wasn't accustomed to pigs, so my first thought was to pick up the little bundle. But instead of being soft and cuddly, he was hard as a stone and very uncooperative, with much thrashing around, accompanied by much squealing. As we really didn't have a place to keep the pig, we just turned him loose and let him socialize with the chickens and the dog, which all went pretty much where they pleased. It wasn't long before Cyrano, as I'd named him, apparently identified with the dog, as he got in the habit of lying under one of the lilac bushes in front of the house on hot afternoons near to where the dog spent his prime loafing time.

Now, all animals believe that to properly loaf it isn't enough to just lie there. They have to dig a bit of a hole or depression first, so their body has a more or less form-fitting place to reside. Spud, the dog, had it down pat, and had his hole refined to perfection. After a week or two I noticed the pig had his own special spot, which he spent a considerable amount of time refining.

Life was good.

Time went by this summer of warm breezes and cool rains, and Cyrano soon grew as big as the dog, who weighed forty-five pounds. Cyrano's hole under the bush increased proportionately. They had evidently become pals, even though the pig was a bit standoffish. I frequently saw them around the farmplace together, and they rarely got into it unless there was some tasty morsel, which they would bicker over with a lot of stiffness, growling and grunting but with no harm really done.

We lived at the end of a road so there wasn't much traffic, but sometimes people did come to see us and they always received an enthusiastic greeting from the dog, as he loved to chase cars. He would hear a car coming and greet it with much barking, tire-biting and general ruckus. As a result, we were rarely surprised by guests.

After a couple of months of watching this, Cyrano apparently thought this was one of his duties—or maybe it was just for fun—to join in on the car chasing. Now when someone came by they would be accompanied by a dog *and* a pig, barking, grunting, growling and biting tires right up to the front door. It was only the truly courageous souls who had the nerve to get out of the car and face all of this fervor without first being reassured by Mom or Dad that it was, "Okay, but watch the pig, he has a bit of an attitude."

Try as we might, we never could break the dog or the pig of this nasty habit, and as summer went along Cyrano turned into quite a speedster.

By fall Cyrano was getting to be a big boy. My dad guessed him at one hundred and fifty pounds, and he knew it. Also, there was a hundred-and-fifty-pound hole under the lilac bush, and I think the bush was starting to lean.

When Spud and Cyrano had a little flare-up it was still pretty much an even match. The pig was much bigger, but Spud had sharp teeth and Cyrano had tender ears.

Fall passed and winter came, and everything slowed down. Cyrano spent the nights on the straw in the barn and Spud spent the nights in the house. Cyrano hung around the front door a lot during the days. I think he wanted in the house, too. Mom was not pleased.

With the warm spring days, everything returned to the good-weather mode. The chickens ate everything green that poked out of the ground, the cows got off their diet of hay and returned to the pasture, and Cyrano, who weighed about three hundred pounds, returned to his lilac bush. All the trees and bushes began to leaf out except, conspicuously, the pig's bush. It had, apparently, taken all the abuse it could stand and had expired over the winter. Cyrano, realizing that this collection of twigs would never keep the harsh summer sun off his delicate skin, promptly started excavating a new hole under a different bush.

Within two days he'd dug a hole you could have hidden a small car in. It looked like a bunker from World War I.

Mom was not happy. The pig had to go.

All my whining was to no avail. They decided to take the pig to the sale barn and let someone else deal with him. Dad didn't have a truck to haul him, and it would be too expensive to hire someone to haul a single pig to the sale, so he decided to do the hauling himself in the panel truck.

To those of you who don't know what a panel truck is, it's very much like an early Suburban, but without some of the luxury items such as cruise control, air conditioning and glass in the passenger-side door.

Getting Cyrano into the panel truck turned out to be very tricky. Lassoing him did not work as he had a very short, fat neck and was much too crafty to let that happen. Chasing him down was useless because he was fast as greased lightning. And even if we did catch him, he outweighed Dad by a hundred pounds and Dad wasn't fond of the idea of being bitten or trampled by a pig. The only thing left was to resort to wit. Yes, sneakiness. After all, we were smarter than the pig.

Dad opened the back doors of the panel truck and built a little ramp so it would be easy for Cyrano to get in, as he surely would since he got into everything else on the place. All we had to do was watch, and then when he was lounging in there we would slam the doors and off we would go. It was a good plan, but as the days went by it seemed like it was taking a long time to mature. The pig checked out the truck thoroughly but would have nothing to do with our scheme. And, as this was Dad's work truck, it was causing him a great inconvenience.

We had to be sneakier.

There was nothing Cyrano liked more than apples. Dad decided he would place a half dozen apples in the truck where he was sure the pig would see. Cyrano would be unable to resist the apples. Surely he would jump in the back. Then we would slam the doors and off we would go! Resolution.

We attracted Cyrano's attention by playing a game of catch by the truck. As always, if there was anything going on, the pig would give it a thorough inspection. Cyrano showed up to see what gives.

Dad quickly placed some apples in the panel truck, and Cyrano gave them the eyeball. Then he gave Dad the eyeball. Then he gave the apples the eyeball. It was crunch time. Like a speeding freight train the pig was in the truck, and we slammed the doors.

Ah, the sweet smell of success!

We raced to the front, opened the doors to pile in and lo and behold there was Cyrano in the front seat, tail twitching and nose-hair bristling with attitude. He had eaten all six apples and crawled over the front seat in ten seconds. The jig was up. Cyrano knew something smelled in Denmark as well as in the panel truck.

Dad had a kind of dejected look on his face as he realized the pig had once again come out on top of things. He said, "Looks like we'll have to try something else," and walked off.

The next day the truck was empty and Cyrano was gone. Two more days went by and not a sign. The third day our neighbor, who lived down the hill by the river and who had a menagerie of normal as well as misfit animals, called and asked if we were missing a pig.

Mom said no.

Marshall Anderson is a singer, songwriter and musician, but on those frozen winter nights when the north wind howls and the ice crystals beat against the windowpane, the experiences of youth find their way to the written word. You've read one of his stories. To hear his music, go to http://myspace.com/andersondavisband.

Photo provided by Grover Reiser

FUEL

Grover Reiser

I was four years old in the winter of 1951. At that time I had an older brother, Rolland, and two younger brothers. Wade was three and the baby, Curt, was a year old. We lived in rural North Dakota, a few miles from the town of Garrison.

Dad worked at the dam site near Riverdale that winter, about forty miles away. Each week, on Monday morning, he'd walk from the farmhouse we rented, to Garrison. From there he'd catch a ride to Riverdale, staying in a boarding house while he was there. Dad had a 1947 Pontiac, but the country roads weren't plowed and the snow was so deep in places that it reached the tops of the telephone poles. The car, snowed in at the farmhouse, was useless to any of us.

Mom, my brothers and I got along as best we could on our own during the week.

We had no phone, no way to communicate with the outside world. The house had no electricity or running water. We had an outhouse, to which we kept a pathway shoveled. We had a well for water, with a hand pump in the kitchen. The cookstove took either wood or coal, and Mom would heat water on the stove for cooking, washing dishes and bathing. We bathed in a round metal washtub in the kitchen, the youngest going first and then on up to the oldest, all using the same water. Mom scrubbed clothes by hand in the same tub, using a washboard.

We also had a radio, which was powered by a small wind charger on the roof of the house. If the wind was blowing it produced enough electricity for the radio or one light bulb. On Saturday nights Dad would sit close to the radio and listen to the *Grand Ole Opry*.

In the main room there was a potbellied stove that heated the entire house. It also took either coal or wood. In the fall a couple of tons of coal would be delivered to the farmhouse and dumped in a big pile outside. We kids would be dispatched to go out and get chunks of coal to burn in the stove.

Every Friday, when it was time for Dad to come home, Mom bundled Rolland and me up in our winter clothes. Pulling our bobsled, we'd head out to meet Dad as he headed back to us with a couple of gunnysacks full of groceries. Usually he brought eggs, milk, and some canned goods. We'd meet him about halfway. He'd place the gunnysacks on the bobsled, put Rolland and me on there as well, and pull the loaded sled the rest of the way home. One time when we got back to the farmhouse all the eggs were broken. This didn't go over well with Mom.

Walking to meet Dad was something of an adventure for Rolland and me. It got us away from the farmhouse each week, even if only for a couple of hours.

But Rolland could be ruthless, and if I lagged behind he wouldn't wait for me. I remember one Friday, as we headed out to meet Dad, one of my legs broke through the surface crust and plunged deep into the snow. I was stuck. Try as I might, I couldn't pull myself free. I called out for Rolland to help me.

Instead, he left me behind.

I cried, stuck there in the snow. I was sure I'd never get out again, thought I was going to die right there on the side of the road. I was still crying an hour later when Rolland and Dad made their return trip. Dad pulled me free with very little effort, it seemed, plopped me down on the bob-sled next to a grinning Rolland, and we headed for the house.

That winter was especially harsh, the worst one I re-member. We had several snowstorms, one after the other, and every day the snow accumulated. We were increasingly isolated.

Rolland and I usually managed to make our own fun. A huge snowdrift had gathered beside the calf barn. We would walk up that drift to the roof of the barn, then we'd slide all the way down. Mom would get mad and tell us to stop, but as soon as she was busy with Wade and Curt we'd be back at it.

As the snow piled up, it became increasingly difficult for Dad to get home on the weekends. Without even a telephone, Mom had no one to talk to other than us kids.

Mom kept potatoes in the root cellar, as well as canned goods. In the fall she'd canned a hundred chickens. Food wasn't an issue.

But the cold was.

We'd been snowed in—and Dad out—for a few weeks when we ran out of coal to heat the house. The house wasn't insulated, and was so drafty we could feel the wind coming in through the walls.

Mom was forced to start breaking up the furniture to put into the potbellied stove. First she broke apart the sofa with a hammer, then she took the ax to it. She then fed it, piece by piece, to the potbellied stove.

Next went the chairs. When those were gone, she went outside and pulled up fence posts, chopped them up and burned them, as well.

As Mom was outside pulling yet another fence post, we kids were at the window in the main room, watching her. Curt's crib was in that room. I was in the crib with Curt, also trying to see out the window.

Then Rolland, standing on Mom's treadle sewing machine, lost his balance and fell against the window. It broke, cutting his arm. The cut bled profusely, and Rolland started crying.

Wade, frightened by the noise, also began crying, and when Curt joined in I decided it was time to bail out of the crib. But as I tried to climb out, I fell.

For some reason, there was a hooked finishing nail sticking out of the side of the crib. That nail caught on my butt cheek through my pants and I dangled there, suspended in mid-air. I wailed with the rest of them.

Mom came in from outside, stood in the doorway and took in this scene of chaos—Rolland bleeding, me hanging by the skin of my butt, all of us crying, blood everywhere. It was too much for her. Mom began to cry as well.

The mutual misery didn't last long. Mom soon pulled herself together. She got everyone settled down, bandaged up and fed.

Once order had been restored, Mom went back outside. She gathered some coal dust—all that was left of our fall delivery—and got busy. With the coal dust she wrote FUEL in huge letters in the snow.

As was her intention, an airplane flying overhead eventually spotted her message, for a couple of days later an "Army Weasel" rumbled up to the farmhouse on rolling tracks. The Army Weasel looked like a tank, but without the gun in front. In it were two uniformed National Guardsmen and a nurse, the latter complete with white dress and starched white cap.

The men unloaded gunnysacks of coal and food for us. The nurse came into the house, checked everyone out to make sure we were all healthy and not in immediate danger of perishing. My brothers and I thought of it as just another adventure.

The guardsmen and the nurse stayed for only a short while, just long enough to give us what we'd need to survive on our own a bit longer.

Dad was able to make it home again a few days later, but that winter was the final straw for my mother. As soon as spring rolled around and the snow melted, she packed us up and we moved away from that farmhouse.

We survived the winter of '51, though with considerably less furniture than we'd started out with.

Grover Reiser has been a truck driver for more than thirty-five years. He grew up in small towns in North Dakota and Minnesota, and now lives in a small town in Iowa.

Photo provided by Betty Hembd Taylor

STARS IN THE WINDOW

Betty Hembd Taylor

Whenever we had a family picture taken between the years 1941 and 1945, my mother would insist that we stand outside under the big double windows so the flags there would be in the picture. The United States government supplied the flags to the families of servicemen and women, as symbols of those in uniform.

Two such flags hung in the windows of our farmhouse, near a little Iowa town called Ocheyedan.

One flag had a single star with a golden fringe. It was an overseas flag, representing my oldest brother, Bob. He'd been serving a one-year tour of duty with the National Guard, beginning in March of 1941. But three-fourths of the way through his year the Japanese bombed Pearl Harbor, and the country was at war. The United States declared war on Japan, and Germany and Italy declared war on the United States. Tours of duty were reclassified, and changed to "for the duration of the War plus six months."

At age six, I found much of what was occurring in the world unclear and mysterious. My parents spoke about the war in serious, hushed tones and speculated about where Bob would be sent. During the next years his letters would often arrive with a New York postmark, and large sections inked out or cut out. My mother said that meant my brother was in the European theater of the war.

Bob's tour of duty led him to Ireland, Africa, and Italy, serving under Generals George Patton and Mark Clark.

When he was moved from one place to another his letters came postmarked, "Somewhere in . . . " My worried parents predicted where he might be going next. They were always right, and I could not figure out how they knew. Edward R. Murrow's broadcasts and Ernie Pyle's columns were relatively unknown to me.

The other flag had two stars. It didn't have a golden fringe, because those it represented were not serving outside the United States. One star stood for my brother Arnold, and the other for his wife, Bonnie. Arnold had been drafted after the conflict began. He was trained to take code as a radio operator in the newly formed Army Air Force. Arnold was naturally left-handed, and he often spoke of the confusion he dealt with, as regulations required that he tap out codes only with his right hand.

Arnold was stationed in several different places, from Florida to California. For a while he was stationed at the air base in Sioux Falls, just sixty-five miles from home. He came home frequently, whenever he had a weekend pass. During the time he was in Sioux Falls he married Bonnie, his hometown sweetheart. Bonnie had been a school-teacher, but determined that if her husband were to be in the service, she would be, too. She joined the WAVES and wore her uniform with pride. She trained and served as an airplane mechanic. I was the only one of my friends who had a sister-in-law, and I was pretty conceited about her being in the service and being a mechanic to boot. Later they were both stationed near San Francisco, and could spend weekend passes together.

My parents worried a lot about Arnold being in California, because they knew he might be sent somewhere in the Pacific. They were of the opinion that the Pacific was even worse than Europe, that we did not understand the Japanese way of fighting, and such diseases as malaria, jungle rot or yellow fever surely awaited Arnold if he should be sent overseas. Miraculously, he never had to go.

My most disturbing childhood memory is of coming home from school to find my mother weeping over a letter from someone whose only presence was represented by a star in the window.

My father's family wrote a "round robin." This was a collection of letters, sent from one family to another among his eleven living siblings, scattered across the country from Wisconsin to California. When the letters arrived at our house we read them thoroughly. Then my father would take out his old letter, add a new one, and send the "robin" on its way. Through these letters I got to know aunts and uncles I'd never met in person. Among the letters there would often be photographs of cousins in uniform, sometimes as many as twenty or more pictures. Though I didn't know them personally, I was proud of them all.

Through the letters my parents learned that a cousin from Montana was stationed in Italy during the same time Bob was there. They passed that information on to my brother, and the two young soldiers were able to find each other and meet for the first time. Far away from either of their homes, a friendship formed that would last throughout their lives.

Years later, I began to comprehend the dangers these young soldiers had faced, and marveled that not one of them had been killed or seriously wounded. Once Bob did receive a surface wound from a piece of shrapnel, but he refused the Purple Heart because he didn't want to worry our parents. One cousin came home from the Philippines with malaria, and my state-bound brother had lifelong problems with a foot that was not properly cared for after a service-connected injury, but there were no war casualties.

Those were days of heart-felt patriotism, with flag waving, ration stamps and War Bonds. I used to save pennies to buy twenty-five cent stamps to put in a book. When I had $18.75 worth of stamps, I could trade the book for a bond that would be worth $25 in ten years.

Recycling was a national passion. We saved tinfoil from gum wrappers, washed and crushed tin cans, collected milkweed pods for life jackets and planted Victory Gardens. My favorite aunt worked in a defense plant in Minneapolis.

Marijuana, which had been eradicated from roadside ditches, was reintroduced and renamed hemp. Its fibers were used for the manufacture of rope and twine, since the import of sisal from other countries was hampered by the war. Hogs noted for their fat were in demand, as the lard was used for munitions.

Gasoline and tire rationing dictated that family outings were infrequent, and a bit of an endurance test. The speed limit was 35 miles per hour, which almost everyone observed as the slower speed saved gas and tires. Twice a year we went to Lake Okoboji, twenty-five miles from home. One time was for the Sunday-School picnic and the other was for the Farm Bureau picnic.

On the way home we sometimes picked up hitchhiking soldiers and took them as far as Ocheyedan, where they hoped to pick up other rides to get them back to the Sioux Falls Airbase. I'm certain my parents would have been leery of hitchhikers before and after the war, but during wartime the situation was different. That might have been one of their boys on the side of the road.

On Saturday nights the neighbors gathered in town to buy groceries, get haircuts, fill cars with gas and visit with friends. During that time my mother, with a group of Red Cross volunteers, folded bandages for servicemen. Sometimes there would be free movies shown outside, in a vacant lot beside the new town hall that had been built by WPA workers just before the war. The lumberyard had provided planks and cement blocks for seating in that outdoor theater.

Besides gas and tires, many other things were in short supply. We needed ration stamps for such things as coffee, sugar and shoes. Like all of our neighbors who survived the Depression, my parents did not regard the stamps as an impossible hardship.

It was during those years that I received my greatest lesson in honesty. Each member of the family was allowed enough stamps to buy two pairs of shoes annually. Once my mother took me to buy a pair of shoes. After we left the store, she discovered the clerk had forgotten to take her ration stamp. Without a moment's hesitation, she went back into the store and handed the stamp to the startled clerk. I hold that enduring vision of my mother, and to this day I can't keep an extra nickel if someone gives me too much change.

Having an airbase so near provided a special treat for students in our little rural school. Often the pilots would fly in formation overhead. At the sound of the planes, we would look expectantly at our teacher. At her nod of approval we all trooped out through the school door to watch the planes flying high above us.

When Germany signed the terms for unconditional surrender, the director of our school came to make the announcement in person, and school was dismissed for the day in celebration. Everyone was jubilant.

Some time passed before our little community transitioned to peace. Servicemen and women did not return overnight. Some came back changed, and some did not come back at all.

One summer day in 1945, some of my siblings and I went to town with our mother. When we returned our father came running down the drive to meet us. He grabbed the door handle and raced alongside the car, laughing as he ran.

Our mother assumed he was up to some nonsense and was annoyed with him, but then he opened the door and exulted, "Bob is on his way home!" The mailman had returned a letter she had mailed to Bob, and he was indeed returning from the war.

I don't remember how much time passed before Bob came home, but I do remember meeting the train in Ocheyedan and seeing his smile as he walked toward us. I was six years old when he left, and nearing my eleventh birthday when he returned. Bonnie had already been discharged and was about to give birth to my first nephew. Arnold did not receive his discharge until after we entered the nuclear age and Japan had surrendered uncond-itionally.

The world was changed, and the little town of Ocheyedan celebrated. Most of the soldiers from Europe were home, and they reveled most of all. I was awed by the parades, ceremonies, and dancing.

My mother's private ceremony was to take the flags from the window and, with joy and relief, put them away. A few months later, Arnold and Bonnie came home. They brought my nephew with them. Life was good, Depression days were over, rationing was over, the war was behind us. It seemed peace would last forever.

And I was the only one in my grade who was an aunt.

Betty Hembd Taylor is a mother, grandmother and retired teacher. She lives in Hartley, Iowa where she and her husband once operated an antique shop and continue to sell at flea markets. She coordinates a writing group at the local library.

GROWING UP GERMAN

Arlene Walker

Most children living on farms in the 1940s attended one-room country schools. All eight grades were taught by one teacher. Each grade took turns going to the front of the room and sitting on a long recitation bench for class, the youngest students usually being first. Meanwhile, students not in class were expected to complete assignments independently at their desks.

I was almost five when my parents prepared me for school. Dad bought a legal-sized, Red Chief tablet and Mom sharpened a wooden pencil with a paring knife. As I sat on my knees at the kitchen table, Dad showed me how to print my name. Mom had sewn new cotton dresses for me, and on the first day Dad drove me to my school two miles from our farm.

One barrier stood between the other students and me— I was not fluent in English. My dad, my mom's parents and other people living in our community were immigrants from Ostfriesland in northern Germany, and spoke *Plattdeutsch**.

Wanting to speak English, I listened, watched other students, and paid attention to my teachers.

Most teachers were strict, demanding good behavior and promptness. That meant no gum chewing, no whispering during school, and getting assignments done on time. The punishment for not obeying the rules was having to stay in at recess.

The events of World War II permeated our lives. For one thing, there was a shortage of certain supplies. Coupon books were issued to every person, limiting purchases of certain food items, clothing, rubber tires, and gasoline.

One teacher led us on regular hikes through roadside ditches to gather milkweed pods. These were sent to a location where the floss—the inside white fibers connected to the seeds—was removed and used as stuffing in life preserver vests for servicemen.

We heard tragic war reports on the radio. While Dad read *The Des Moines Tribune*, I studied the photos on the newspaper's pages. I learned to recognize President Roosevelt, and the thin-faced, angry man with a mustache named Adolf Hitler.

Though not much was said in my school about the war, an incident happened one day that has remained in my memory. I had to stay in at recess to finish my arithmetic problems. After the teacher and most of the students had gone outside, I looked up from my work to see an older boy drawing huge swastikas on the blackboard. *Why is he drawing those awful symbols that we all associate with Hitler?* I wondered.

As though he had read my mind, the boy turned. The angry look in his eyes as they met mine signaled a piercing hatred for me. Emphasizing his look, he pointed an accusing finger in my direction, sending a chill of fear through me.

At home, Dad and Mom sat by the kitchen table drinking their afternoon tea when I told them what had happened at school. Their expressions showed concern. That day I learned that Americans whose ancestors had lived in the United States for a long time hated Germans who were recent immigrants. It didn't seem to matter to them that my grandparents and my dad had acclimated to U.S. culture by learning the language, becoming citizens, and showing loyalty to the U.S. flag.

I'm sure my parents felt the pain of rejection even more than I did. Yet they went on with their work on the farm and the care of their family. Our days were mixed with both happiness and sadness. Letters from Dad's family in Germany were censored and resealed before they reached our mailbox.

Drinking tea in mid-afternoon was a custom Low Germans brought from the "Old Country." This was when Dad read and interpreted the German letters written in *Hochdeutsch*** to Mom while we children listened. One letter brought the news that Dad's brother was killed in battle. Later, Dad read a letter telling of another brother taken prisoner by enemy troops. And a letter causing tears to form in Dad's eyes told us that his mother, the grandmother I never met, had died after an illness.

Toward the end of the war we learned that the effects of war had produced great poverty in Germany. Our relatives lacked food and other basic supplies. From a trip to town Dad brought home eight empty boxes and food supplies. Each box was addressed to our family members in need. Mom sewed small muslin bags that were stronger than the cellophane that packaged rice, sugar, coffee, and tea. The muslin bags would not break open easily while jostled on the trip across the ocean. If there were any spaces left in the boxes they were stuffed with shoes, clothes, or treats such as chewing gum and hard candy.

Sometimes more than a month passed before we heard from the recipients of the packages. Letters from Germany were always picked up first from the stack of mail. Mom used a paring knife as a letter opener, being careful not to tear any corners of the thin, crisp airmail paper. We all listened as Dad read the words of thanks that uncles and aunts expressed for the supplies they had received from us. Sometimes they sent photos of themselves or their children, our cousins. It gave us satisfaction to have given to family members in need.

In 1962, Dad and Mom flew to Dad's homeland. Having been separated from his family for thirty-nine years, Dad, with Mom joining in, celebrated a tearful reunion with relatives. An expression of the relatives' gratefulness was a bouquet of twenty-nine pink carnations, which Mom carried off the plane when my brother and I met them at the airport on their return.

My siblings and I have made trips to Ostfriesland, walked the streets Dad walked as a boy, and visited the home where he grew up. While enjoying afternoon tea in the homes of cousins, we tried to recall and converse in *Plattdeutsch*. No one laughed at our faulty attempts, and the stories and laughter we shared bonded us together as family.

I'm thankful for the sacrifices made by my parents so that my siblings and I could have opportunities they had not been granted. Dad and Mom encouraged me, and helped me get an education so I could live my dream of becoming a teacher.

My own struggles in learning English and adapting to American culture enabled me later to show compassion and understanding for my students, especially the children of immigrants in my classes.

I'm proud to be an American, and treasure the experience of growing up German.

Plattdeutsch, or Low German, refers to various dialects spoken in northern Germany.
**Hochdeutsch*, or High German, is spoken in southern Germany. It is the standard German language taught in schools.

Arlene Walker has taught elementary classrooms, English Language Learners and has been a substitute teacher. She lives in Sanborn, Iowa, and enjoys reading, cooking, quilting and walking.

POTATOES *MIT* GRAVY

C.R. Lindemer

When I recall my German grandmother, Kathrine, it's never without the memory of how she clung to one precious preposition and the dear German conjunctions. Her thick accent would never leave her, and she did not appear to notice or care.

The dinner table is where I recall the German "little words," as they nearly always came up, because bread and potatoes were common elements of the hearty basic meals my German grandmother always made. You would never be asked about potatoes with gravy or potatoes with butter. It was always "potatoes *mit* gravy." That delicious, every-day gravy was made with the addition of the milky potato water. If you didn't want gravy, the "or butter" option would be your obvious choice. "How about some more potatoes *mit* gravy?" Grandma would often ask. "*Oder* butter?" And you might want some bread and butter on the side. "Some bread *und* butter?" she would inquire.

My grandparents allowed me to mix all of my food together: meat, boiled potatoes, fresh steamed cabbage, and cultured butter in a winding, circular pattern on my thick, plain white German plate. They never seemed to mind my lunchtime cyclone-on-a-plate. The small pieces were all there and the way they fit together didn't matter to them.

Nobody ever corrected Grandma, because everyone understood her. The little words didn't matter that much in a sense, as long as all of the other words worked together. They didn't speak German in the home, with the exception of the precious preposition and dear conjunctions. But Grandpa did sing "O Tannenbaum" at Christmas, which is why I can still sing it from memory.

I don't recall my German grandfather, Carl, clinging so strongly to the same small German words. He was a calm, quiet man who drove a small gray "putt-putt" Ford tractor, always far below the posted speed limit. He would feign delight at each perennial batch of kittens on our farm, not even a mile northeast of his. Grandpa was a man of few words, including prepositions and conjunctions.

Their language was a dialect of *Plattdeutsch*, the parlance of the "low country" in northern Germany. It was the language of the country, of the village, the farmers, and of the low, flat tulip fields with their long, straight rows of rainbow colors. My grandparents chose to lose their *Plattdeutsch* as they tried to fit into the rural Midwestern countryside. They didn't want to be just Germans anymore. They wanted to be English-speaking American landowners.

They had left their mothers and their fathers, their brothers and their sisters, villages, their country, their language, and last of all, the German voices of the people who were ever dear to them in the country of the only language they ever really knew. And though she learned the basics of English, Grandma would always hold onto the precious preposition and the dear conjunctions.

My memories of my German grandparents are always melded with the image of my grandmother in a faded housedress, decked with a full-length floral print apron with gigantic pockets. Her image is laced with the yeasty smell of warm bread dough rising in steel breadboxes, combined with faint traces of damp black earth and small bits of manure tracked in from the farmyard. The bread was her mother's recipe, brought over from Germany, not written on paper but in Grandma's mind and in her heart.

They were two strong American farmers, Kathrine *und* Carl, from the "Old Country, Deutschland." They were in America *mit* nothing but each other and a tractor and a plow and the will to succeed, with a wish *und* a solemn prayer.

C. R. Lindemer grew up on a Minnesota dairy farm and lives with her family on an historic farmstead in Groton, Massachusetts. She is the sole proprietor of Boston Road Communications.

WHAT DID YOU SAY?

Joanne Dyhrkopp Schar

Back when I was a kid, my Grandpa Lindgren had a friend, Harold O. Nelson, who had come over from the "Old Country" in his youth. Harold O. would come to the farm when a heifer got into the alfalfa and bloated, or when they took care of pigs. Grandpa would take me with him to Harold O.'s farm when Harold needed help dehorning steers.

I really liked Harold O. and his wife, Ethel. Harold was short and filled out his blue overalls like Tweedle-Dee. Ethel was tall and raw-boned, and wore her hair in the traditional braids pinned in circles on her head. They were nice, friendly folks, but the thing that attracted me to them was their old country accents. The soft brogue of Malmo was one of the last remnants of Sweden left to them after more than thirty years of life in western Iowa. I loved the sounds of English sung in that particular Scandinavian way. At age seven I had a good ear for speech patterns and enjoyed copying the sounds I heard.

One day, when I went to fetch the old workhorse, Boots, from the pasture, I noticed she was walking with a limp. I led Boots to the barnyard to show Grandpa, and he called Harold O., who had cared for his own teams of workhorses for years. In the early '50s farmers only called the vet if the breed bull was dying.

I led Boots to the orchard so I could reach the hose to run some water into a bucket. Then I washed and curried the old horse while we waited for Harold. I asked Grandma for some ribbons to tie in Boots's mane, to decorate her like the horses I had seen at the Monona County Fair. When I finished my handiwork, eight thick braids were tied with the colorful ribbons.

Soon Harold O. drove up in his old 1940s Chevy pickup. After his usual friendly greetings, he walked up to Boots, speaking in a soft, soothing voice. He lifted the offending leg and examined the hoof. Harold had brought a hoof knife, which had a sharp, curved blade. Boots jerked her head up when the sharp knife found a sensitive spot, and I struggled to hold the rope with my two small hands as Grandpa held onto the halter. A black, infected fluid spurted forth. Harold O. let go of the leg and talked softly to Boots as he felt the knee and fetlock. Then he picked up the hoof again and scraped carefully to expose a small jagged rock wedged tightly in there. He flicked the rock to the ground and cleaned the wound with warm, soapy water that Grandma had brought from the kitchen. Then Grandpa poured kerosene into the cut and the hoof met the ground again.

Holding the rope, I led Boots around in a circle so Harold could watch her walk. By the change in her gait it was evident that Boots already felt some relief.

Harold smiled at me, eyed the braided mane, and said, "Dat looks so purrdy."

I beamed and smiled back at him, and said, "It sure is purrdy."

Grandpa Lindgren glared at me over Harold's shoulder. I was confused by the look on his face.

Still looking at the horse, Harold O. said, "Boots needs da udder hoofs trimmed soon, Emil. I'll be back next week ta do it, jah?" He looked at me again and said, "Yup, you take good care of dat horse now." Then he got in his truck, and with a wave, drove down the lane.

Grandpa continued to look at me with rare sternness. He said, " Well, Joanne, what did you say when you were talking to Harold O.? I will not have you making fun of my friend."

"But Grandpa, I don't know what you mean," I replied, my lower lip trembling slightly. "I like Harold O. He's real nice and he fixed Boots. And Boots does look purrdy, now that I tied the ribbons in her mane."

Grandpa just sighed, shook his head and with a wry smile said, "Jah sure, you betcha." He had decided just to let me be a kid, unaware of the pitfalls of mimicry.

Joanne Dyhrkopp Schar lives in Spencer, Iowa, where she was born and raised. When she was young she spent her summers on the farm of her grandparents, Emil and Bessie Lindgren, near the town of Moorhead, Iowa.

Photo provided by Betty Hembd Taylor

STARTING SCHOOL IN THE THIRD GRADE

Peter Davidson

I grew up on a farm in southwest Minnesota. For many years prior to my entering school, farm kids attended country school through eighth grade and then went to town school for grades nine through twelve.

When I was a child, though, farms were becoming larger, which meant there were fewer farm families and thus fewer farm kids for the country schools. Also, some farm families were starting to send their kids to the elementary school in town where they thought they would get a better education than in a one-room country schoolhouse. The days of the one-room country schoolhouse were numbered.

It was obvious that the country school serving our rural township was on the brink of collapse because of declining enrollment.

The teacher had a two-year teaching certificate, which was grandfathered in and was permissible for teaching in a country school, but a four year degree was required by the school board to teach in the town school that served our community. Thus, when her country school closed down, she would be out of a job. The country schoolteacher therefore took matters into her own hands to keep the school open as long as possible—she recruited students.

When I was barely four years old, the country schoolteacher paid a visit to my parents. She looked me over, asked me a couple of questions, sized me up, and pronounced me big enough, old enough, and smart enough to start school in the fall—none of which, by the way, were even close to being accurate. Since there was no kindergarten in country schools, I would go directly into first grade. My parents came from the old school where a teacher was respected and trusted and whatever the teacher said was accepted as the gospel.

So, off to school it was.

There were three of us in the first grade and another five students in grades two through eight. Not a big enough student body to field a baseball team, but big enough to keep the doors open at least one or two more years.

The other students in the first grade were evenly divided between boys and girls—one of each. I had seen the girl somewhere before but had never laid eyes on the boy. I was dutifully impressed, though, when his dad dragged the kicking and screaming boy into the schoolhouse by the ear. In the other hand, the one that wasn't holding onto the ear, the dad carried a sawed-off boat oar about three feet long with a crack in it.

He handed the boat oar to the teacher and said, "Don't be afraid to use this on him if he gets out of line."

I remember very little about country school except that the boy, Harold, was the meanest, nastiest, orneriest, lyingest little . . . uh, guy that I've ever seen. Through the years I have occasionally pondered the chicken and egg theory as it pertains to Harold. You know, which came first, the chicken or the egg? In Harold's case I wonder which came first, the nastiness or the boat oar?

My only vivid recollection of the girl is that I had a nice red ball to play with during recess and that she kicked me in the stomach and took the ball away from me.

When I was in second grade there were only three students in the whole school and it folded after that year.

I entered town school in the third grade and made a huge discovery—the rest of the students in my class could read and print and they were starting to write in cursive.

It was finally discovered that while the country schoolteacher kept the doors open those extra two years, she had actually quit teaching the fall that I'd entered first grade. I built a birdhouse, I recall, and played a lot of games, but we didn't get into the academics.

I had a lot of ground to make up, but with noontime tutoring from my older brother and nighttime tutoring from my mother, I finally caught up with most of them by the end of the fourth grade.

After high school I earned bachelor's and master's degrees and completed an additional year of post-graduate study. I've had successful careers in several disciplines, have written books, magazine articles, short stories, and songs, and have presented writers' seminars in a 15-state area.

I sometimes wonder what I might have accomplished if I hadn't started school in the third grade.

Peter Davidson is the author of twenty-three books published by McGraw-Hill Book Company, Perigee/Putnam Publishers, Haworth Press and others. He has presented more than 600 writers' seminars and has appeared on more than 85 radio and television programs nationwide.

WALKING BEANS WASN'T SOMETHING YOU DID WITH YOUR DOG

THE BILLY GOAT IN THE OUTHOUSE

Tommie L. Haferkamp

Almost every day something happens to remind me of the changes that have taken place since my childhood. Though many of those changes have been to our school system, I do have fond memories of the "good old days," and the following is an account of an incident that happened in 1937, when I was in third grade.

My best friend Bobbie (Bob) and I were inseparable. Her family lived on an adjoining farm. Bob and her younger sister, Billie, always walked with my brother and me to the seven-grade, one-room, one-teacher schoolhouse we attended a mile from our home.

Bob and I had crushes on two seventh-grade boys. No one knew of our imaginary love affairs, especially the boys, but we did a lot of fantasizing as we walked to and from school. We'd walk either behind or ahead of Billie and my brother, so they couldn't overhear us talking about our secret loves.

It was springtime, and the day was beautiful, warm and sunny. Love was flying through the air like the silky seeds of the milkweeds that grew along the edge of the schoolyard. We played "Wolf over the River" during morning recess. It was almost time for the bell to ring when Bob and I decided we needed to answer nature's call before returning to the classroom. The teacher frowned upon pupils who spent the entire recess playing and then raised their hand to be excused as soon as the bell rang.

There were no indoor bathrooms at the school, only outhouses. The girls' outhouse was at the far northwest corner of the playground. It was a "two-holer" with no outside door. I'm not sure why there was no door—perhaps so children wouldn't get locked in or lock others out. The outhouse was U-shaped, with a dividing wall in the middle. There was room for two or three students to wait on one side of the wall, and the holes were on the other side.

Bob and I ran to the outhouse as fast as we could so we wouldn't be tardy when the bell rang. We had almost finished our business when we heard an unusual noise on the other side of the wall. We'd barely gotten our clothes back in place when a huge, mean-looking Billy goat with large horns and a long goatee made his entrance.

Bob and I screamed, climbed on the toilet seat and stood in the far corner. That wasn't easy—there were no covers for the holes, and there was barely room for two little girls to stand without slipping in.

The goat bleated, reared up on his hind legs and put his front hooves on the seat of the toilet. We were frantic and screamed louder, clinging to each other.

After what seemed an eternity, our screaming paid off. Our two seventh-grade heroes came to the rescue. We couldn't believe it when the boys came right inside the girls' toilet!

The horrible goat was led away by our two handsome guys.

Though we were rescued by our idols, Bob and I didn't talk about the day of the Big Bad Billy Goat. We stopped chatting about those two handsome seventh-grade boys. We were humiliated, because they had seen us standing on the seats of the outhouse, yelling for help.

Our embarrassment was even greater when we learned that the goat was a neighbor's pet that was afflicted with spring fever. He had jumped from his pen and had been searching for a pretty little Nanny goat. Instead, he'd found only us.

Bob and her family moved away, and I didn't see her again for several years. But the next time we were together, we had a good laugh about the Billy goat in the outhouse.

Tommie Lee Shults married Verna Haferkamp in 1947 and they had two children, a daughter, Diane, and a son, Lynn. After thirty years of state employment she retired in 1984. Her greatest pleasures these days are her three grandchildren and writing about the "good old days."

Photo provided by Terry Overocker

BORN FREE

Terry Overocker

As a child, books about animals were always my favorites. When I read the book *Born Free*, and saw the TV movie about a couple in Africa raising lion cubs, I was in love. I had to have a lion.

There were so many reasons to get a lion. We had so much wide-open space on our farm, with lots of trees. Our pastures were filled with cattle so food would not be a problem. Water was plentiful. And there were so many lions out there without homes. It was our duty to provide for them.

But my dad just did not understand. My begging and pleading got me nowhere.

Then I saw the movie *Black Beauty*, and I was really in love. My dad must have been feeling guilty about the lion we didn't have because when I told him, "Every girl needs a horse," we started horse shopping.

Our weekends were devoted to finding the perfect horse. We traveled across several counties in search of him or her, looking at horses of every color and size.

Then one Sunday afternoon I found her. Her name was Chris. She was a gray Arabian mare with an extra bonus—she was expecting a foal.

The farm where Chris lived had other horses, but she had her own small pasture. While my parents were talking to the owners, I was sitting on the fence of the pasture watching my horse trot back and forth. During one of her trips around the pasture she looked me right in the eyes. I was spellbound. We were made for each other.

As arrangements were made for Chris's transfer to our farm, I felt that my life was just beginning. I had new roads to travel—on horseback.

School was really interfering with my life. I had a horse. I had no time to go to school. Just try telling that to the board of education!

I awoke before 5:00 a.m. every morning and no longer needed an alarm clock. There was purpose to my life. A reason to get up in the mornings. I had a horse to feed.

Each morning I carried hay and grain from the barn to the pasture. Chris would be waiting for me at the gate of her new pasture. As soon as she saw me she tossed her head and whinnied a loud greeting. While she ate I brushed and combed her, and then climbed on her back.

The world had a whole new perspective from the top of a horse. I was ready to ride. Chris was an excellent teacher. After much slipping and sliding and a few falls, my riding skills improved. We were ready to leave the farm and travel the countryside, exploring new roads.

Chris and I were free spirits. Riding bareback in my bib-overalls and bare feet, with my long hair blowing wildly in the wind and Chris's mane in my face, time ceased to exist.

I was living free.

Terry Overocker lives in a log cabin on the family farm where she grew up. She loves gardening and grows and preserves most of the year's food. She also enjoys music, reading, writing and caring for her family of several cats and a yellow Lab named Sammy.

BEYOND WORDS

Lisa Ohm

On Friday nights there was always a horse auction in that lonely, dilapidated building at the intersection of Highways 9 and 19. There were no advertisements for this event, it was a "word-of-mouth" affair.

Bill Nelson signaled a right turn to go on by, but something made him hesitate. He turned left instead, to the sale barn, parked, and went inside.

"Do I hear twenty-five . . . twenty-five dollars?" the auctioneer barked. "Come on, look at this pretty mare. She's flashy."

Someone yelled back, "Not tonight, she ain't."

Jeers, knee-slaps and claps rippled through the crowd. The "flashy" mare was calm amidst the loud, organized chaos. This caught Bill's eye.

"Do I hear twenty . . . twenty dollars?"

Bill hesitated, then his hand went up. The crowd became interested. They knew this man, and this man knew horses.

"Do I hear twenty-five dollars?"

Another hand shot up. Looks were exchanged.

"Thirty?"

Yep!

"Thirty-five?"

Yep! Heads shook.

I do not need another horse, Bill thought.

The auctioneer's babble between bids ricocheted off the old building's walls. Eyes jumped back and forth between the bidders and the auctioneer. Tension mounted and the bidding continued.

"Going once . . . going twice . . . going three times . . . sold!"

I was just dozing off at the end of a perfect summer day. That afternoon I'd read by the creek while my two brothers had stayed busy swimming and skipping rocks. Now, in my bedroom, I was ready to put the day behind me and looked forward to a peaceful night of dreams. I often dreamt of perfect summer days with the one thing I really wanted—a horse.

But this time my doze was interrupted when the phone downstairs rang. Who would be calling this late at night? I got out of bed and crouched at the top of the stairs to listen.

Mom answered the phone. "You have one horse too many? Oh, Bill, I don't know . . . I guess a look won't hurt. Okay, then, tomorrow morning."

I held my breath. A horse! Silently, I crept back down the hallway, to my room. Sleep didn't come so easily after that.

Early the next day Mom and I drove to Bill Nelson's farm. As Mom and I got out of the Jeep, we saw a mare standing near the pasture fence.

"She's overweight and has a watch-eye," Mom said.

I, on the other hand, saw a perfect horse. She was a beautiful paint mare with a rare watch-eye—blue blending from the pupil into the iris—and a regal stance. A true Picasso on four legs.

Mom put her arm around me and we walked towards Mr. Nelson, already heading to us.

"Why'd you get her?" Mom asked him.

"Had to," was his terse reply.

"You have too many horses already. That doesn't make much sense, Bill."

He paused. "It makes sense."

"Well, do you know anything about her?"

"Nope. The sellers weren't there when she sold."

"Honestly, what do you think?"

Looking right at me, Mr. Nelson said, "I think you have a young girl here who needs this horse."

"Ha! We'll see." Mom looked down at me, then sighed. "I guess I'm out numbered."

"Sold?" Bill asked.

The word hung in the air. I felt like jumping out of my skin.

Looking less than enthusiastic, Mom said, "Sold."

The car ride home was very quiet. Mom kept drumming her fingers nervously on the steering wheel of the old Jeep.

Finally, she broke the silence. "Well, she's ours." She looked over at me. "You gonna help with her?"

"Yes," I promised.

"You gonna ride her, get her in shape?"

"Yes."

"You gonna help with the fencing and feeding?"

"Yes."

"You want to show her?"

"Yes."

"You gonna let me do *all* the talking to your father when we get home?"

"Yes," I promised.

"Okay."

I stared out the window as we drove, grinning beyond ear to ear. Then something dawned on me. I had to ask, "Mom, why'd you pay"—gulp—"a hundred dollars for her?"

". . . had to."

She had to? I sat back. This didn't make sense. Thoughts of Mom's frugal nature came to mind. Memories of washing and drying used plastic baggies, and being lectured about reusing paper lunch bags until they were in shreds came to mind. My brothers and I were constantly reminded to flush the toilet only in the mornings, to save on water. Also: Turn off lights, turn down the heat, five-minute showers, and an inch of water for a bath. And use eggs to wash your hair, not fancy shampoo.

I remembered the Halloween when Mom went ballistic because my older brother dressed up as a robot by wrapping his entire body with all of Mom's Reynolds Wrap. Mom lectured us on the high cost of aluminum foil, and when the robot was disassembled all scraps of the foil that could be salvaged were very carefully cleaned, folded and saved.

What had Mom been thinking by getting this horse? How could we afford a hundred dollars? Finally, I decided I didn't care. We had a beautiful horse. That's what mattered to me.

The horse was delivered to our place the next day. We had a pasture and shelter for her. We borrowed a friend's pony and the pony's foal so the mare wouldn't be lonely. An old bathtub was used as a watering trough.

The horse had no papers, no name, and no information from the auction.

Every Saturday our mother took my brothers and me to the library. Mom loved astrology, I loved Trixie Belden, and my brothers loved riding the elevator. It was April, and taking a cue from her study of astrology, Mom named our horse Aries.

The day came when we finally rode Aries. After putting on a dusty hand-made western saddle, my mom mounted.

With just the lightest cue to move, Aries moved. The mare walked perfectly. She trotted like a ballerina on four legs. She took her leads at the lope like a professional at the World Congress.

Whooping with delight, Mom bent over the saddle and gave Aries a big hug.

She hopped down. "Your turn."

I had been taking riding lessons, but now I hesitated. "Uh . . . okay," I said.

Once I was on Aries, however, I could barely contain my excitement. Holding the reins in my sweaty hands, I looked forward and wrapped my legs around the horse. And then, we moved.

I feel like I'm in a parade, I thought.

I gave the cue for a trot, and again we moved. Aries's trot was smooth and slow. When asked, she trotted out. We slowed to a walk, and then I gave the cue for a lope. Undeniably perfect! Leaning back a little in the saddle was my cue for the horse to stop, and—yes!—the flashy Picasso mare performed flawlessly. She circled, she reversed. I didn't want to get off.

All of this was great in a fenced-in pasture, but I wondered what would happen out on the trail.

The gate opened and Mom called, "When you two get back, walk her out because she'll be sweaty. And don't forget the hug."

Looking up to the sky, I mouthed, "Thank you."

"What do you think?"

I looked up from my homework and saw my first show clothes. I had known something was up. Mom had been sewing like a fiend for days.

"The first show is in two weeks," she said. She held up a pair of shiny riding boots. "Dad bought these."

New boots! I never got anything new. I always got hand-me-downs.

"Well, try them on," she said.

I pulled the boots on. They fit good. They *felt* good. "Um, Mom, they're great. But I need a hat."

"I know," Mom said.

Right then two hooligans burst into the kitchen. My brothers. The younger one, still trying to catch his breath, let the older one do the talking. "Hey, we were just on that horse," he said. "She's fun!"

"What!" I yelled.

"Wild horse!" my brother yelled back.

"What did you two do?" inquired our mother through clenched teeth.

Finding his breath, my younger brother piped in. "We just hopped up on her and rode around the pasture. We used a halter and lead rope. Geez, what's the problem?"

"All of you, down to the barn." Our mother looked none too amused.

I ran down to the barn ahead of them. Mom controlled herself and walked briskly. My brothers, chucking small rocks at each other and unsuspecting birds flying overhead, arrived at the pasture last.

The older one grabbed the halter, walked out to Aries and gently put it on her.

Well, at least he's being nice, I thought.

The younger brother called out impatiently, "Bring her over here."

"Just wait," the other spat back. Using the fence railing, he hopped on. Then the impatient one climbed on behind him.

"Ready?"

Wrapping his arms around his big brother's waist, he nodded his head up and down like a crazy woodpecker. Grinning, they both dug their heels into the horse's sides.

Executing a perfect lope, Aries kindly took the two cowboys around the pasture.

After our dropped jaws and chins were picked up, Mom and I were laughing hard at the sight.

"Mom, this horse is great!" the renegades shouted in unison.

They slid to a stop in front of us.

Trying to maintain some composure, Mom asked, "Did you two know she would ride double, *and* bareback, *and* without a bridle before you did this?"

"No. Geez, were we supposed to ask her?"

At that, the mare slowly turned her neck and looked back at the two boys, then nickered.

There followed years of shows, ribbons, riding double, barefoot, bareback, in the creek, up hills, and anywhere we wanted. There was a lot of talking to and kindness given on my part. So much more, more than that horse could ever know, was given back to me.

Then, as girls do, I grew up. I went off to college. My life took a different direction. The boys were also gone, and Aries was no longer being ridden.

We talked about what to do with Aries. We were very particular about what happened to her. We wanted her to have a good home. Eventually, another family with a young girl and dreams of a perfect summer day that included a horse was found. Our mare moved there.

Thirty years passed. I was grown and had children of my own. Then, by strange coincidence, I found out more about that horse from so long ago.

Living in Minnesota now, I received a phone call from my mother, who had recently relocated back to the town we grew up in in Wisconsin.

Mom said, "You won't believe this. I just learned my neighbor and her father once owned Aries. They were the ones who took her to auction."

The story goes, Aries had a foal, but the foal died. The family decided they couldn't afford the horse any more, so they took her to auction. Bill Nelson bid one hundred dollars because he "had to." My mom paid the same price because she "had to."

Why? Bill Nelson, I was told, had been bidding against the slaughter man. I had been taking riding lessons near the Nelson farm, and he knew of my dreams. Bill saw something special in that mare, and knew who might be a good match for a horse like that.

I know in my heart the day I saw that horse something special happened. Once in a lifetime, maybe twice if extremely lucky, a horse comes along and gives you everything, and I mean everything, she's got.

I realize her gift now. It's beyond words what that mare meant to me.

Lisa Ohm has been a therapeutic horseback riding instructor and Special Olympic Equestrian coach for more than twelve years. She lives with her husband, son, daughter, horses (of course), dogs, cats, barn bunny and chickens in Jordan, Minnesota.

THE GREAT SNOWMAN WAR OF 1952

Margaret Fielding Roberts

I loved winters as a child in Nebraska. I loved the deep, fluffy snow that beckoned and offered so many possibilities for fun.

Every Saturday my two sisters and I jumped out of bed first thing in the morning, then, bundled up in our wool coats, rubber boots and mismatched mittens, we'd head outside. Mom attempted to feed us before we went out the door, but we were usually so eager to go that we'd try to be outside before she knew what we were up to.

As the oldest, I felt it was my privilege to dictate what we would do first. My sisters usually bowed to my authority, though Gloria, younger by two years, sometimes rebelled. She'd spent a good portion of February constructing several snowmen, and she wanted to continue working on them. Snowmen were fine. I enjoyed making them as much as anyone. But our yard was already populated by an entire large family of snowpeople, and the novelty was wearing off.

Nancie, the baby of the family, wanted to work on the snow fort we'd been perfecting, so I decided that's what we'd do that particular Saturday morning. Nancie got busy packing some new snow "bricks" to line the fort, while Gloria and I stacked them, making the wall of the fort taller. Behind the wall was a neat pyramid of snowballs that we'd built and stockpiled. We'd packed the snowballs as firmly as we could, so they were as hard and deadly as small cannonballs.

After a while, we began to wish some neighbor kids would venture near the yard so we could test our snowballs. We crouched behind the wall of our fort, conspiring on how we would launch a surprise attack on anyone careless enough to approach our property.

Unfortunately, no other kids came near.

Gloria was so desperate that she was tempted to launch a snowball at poor old Mrs. Hayslert as she hobbled by on her way to the general store up town, five blocks from our house. I stopped Gloria in time. She sulked. I pointed out to her that if we hit Mrs. Hayslert with a snowball she would certainly tell our mother, who would in turn tell our father, who would probably take a switch to our backsides. Gloria wisely backed off.

When Mom called us in for lunch we reluctantly trudged past our snowmen, to the house. Nancie stopped along the way to straighten the hat of one of the smaller snowpersons, a lopsided creature on which she had placed one of Mom's old Sunday bonnets. We had a box full of discarded hats, scarves and ties that we used to clothe our snowpeople. When Nancie had spotted the pink straw hat with its colorful silk flowers around the rim she'd announced it perfect for her favorite creation.

We gobbled down lunch. Sandwiches on thick, homemade bread and fried potatoes with onions would stick to our ribs for the rest of the afternoon. When we were done we headed for the back door, where our pile of coats, boots and mittens rested in a soggy pile by the heat register.

Nancie was fast and usually managed to get dressed first. She was out the door before Gloria or I had our boots on. We were still inside when we heard Nancie's cry of outrage.

Gloria and I looked at each other, then ran outside to investigate, hopping as we jammed our feet into our boots.

While we'd been eating lunch, three of our snowmen had been slaughtered. Nancie's favorite had been be-headed. The pink straw hat lay several feet away in the snow.

Another snowman, one we'd dressed up with an old shawl, lay on its side. Yet another was facedown.

Who had done this terrible deed? And how had so much destruction been done in such a short time?

We soon had our answer.

Look! Nancie cried, pointing.

In the front yard of the Aronson house, across the street from us, stood a snowman. We were all quite certain that snowman hadn't been there before lunch. We would have noticed.

And it was a truly sinister snowman.

From its sides protruded two crooked branches for arms. At the end of one of the branch-arms hung a BB-gun. The snowman's mouth appeared to be made of the same small pebbles we used for ours, but instead of a smiling mouth, as all our snowmen possessed, this snowman's mouth turned down at the corners. It seemed to sneer.

But the worst part was the helmet that sat on the snowman's head. It was a German war helmet, which we knew because we'd seen similar helmets in the movies we watched on television. Our father loved war movies, and whenever there was one on we were all obliged to watch it with him on the black and white television set in our living room.

As Nancie mourned her fallen snowman, Gloria and I continued to mull over the mystery of how this had been accomplished in the short time we'd been eating lunch.

Then, one of the Aronson kids made an appearance.

We didn't know the Aronsons well, though they lived across the street and some of their kids attended the same school we did. We only knew that there were a bunch of them. This one was tall, his arms so long that his wrists hung bare from the sleeves of his coat. Herb Aronson, sixteen years old, sauntered over to the Nazi-snowman and stood there grinning at us, his arms crossed.

Then the other Aronson siblings appeared, one by one: Gordy, the next in line; Ronald and Rupert, the twins; Albert and Winston, who weren't twins, but who were so close in age that they were in the same grade in school; and Pat, the youngest. We'd heard rumors that Pat was a girl, but we weren't convinced. None of us had ever seen her in a skirt, and her wavy hair was nearly as short as that of her siblings.

All of the Aronson kids were redheaded and freckled, and all possessed sour dispositions and unsavory reputations.

As we watched, they got busy. Before our astonished eyes they created a second snowman in a matter of minutes, in the hand of which they placed a bayonet that looked disturbingly real.

When they started on their third snowman, we realized this was serious.

Gloria, Nancie and I hurried to our snow fort and hunkered down behind it. We were grateful for our hard little pile of snowballs. We only wished we'd made more.

We talked strategy. Gloria and Nancie were all for sending me out to draw the enemies' fire so they could fling snowballs at them. I wasn't crazy about that idea.

We settled instead on pulling in whatever snow we could reach and adding to our snowball pile.

As the afternoon wore on, we finally dared to peek out. The army across the street had grown to an alarming size. There was a motley group of half a dozen snowmen in the Aronson yard. They held guns, knives and even one hatchet. All wore surly scowls. One had an eye-patch, as though already the survivor of battle.

My sisters and I quaked in our boots as we observed this army, but we were careful not to let our fear show.

The first snowball flew, in our direction. It fell short of our fort, but it conveyed a clear message: This was war.

Possessing the strongest arms, Gloria and I threw snowballs as hard as we could while Nancie scrambled to create more ammo. In return, the Aronson clan threw their snowballs at us. In spite of being mostly older and bigger, their aim wasn't as good, and we had the advantage of having our fort to hide behind, while they stood out in the open.

It didn't take long for them to figure it out, though, and soon the Aronson twins went to work creating a fort for their side.

Nancie, industrious as ever, scrambled away from our spot just long enough to scoop up some rocks from around the base of a nearby Dutch elm tree. She packed snow around the rocks, creating more deadly snowballs to add to our pile.

The battle went on for a while, without much real damage being done. I did manage to hit Pat Aronson on the leg at one point. She yelped—a satisfying sound if ever there was one—and threw a wildly off-target snowball in response.

Then things turned ugly. Realizing they weren't having much luck reaching us with their snowballs, the Aronsons took aim at our snowpeople, instead. This made sense. It had been an attack on one of our own that had started this whole ruckus in the first place. But when Rupert Aronson— or maybe it was Ronald, we weren't sure—threw a snowball that hit one of Gloria's favorite snowmen, we were outraged. That snowman was the one our father had jokingly dubbed "Uncle Milty" because of its protruding chest, over which we'd draped a flowered shawl. When hit it toppled over, the top two sections breaking away from the base, and lay there like the victim of some terrible crime.

We renewed a flurry of angry volleys, but hesitant to come out from behind our fort, our attack was ineffectual.

Next to fall was one of my own creations, a snowman I'd built and was especially proud of for its nearly perfect, picture-book form. I'd wrapped a scarf around its neck and had talked our mother out of a fresh carrot for its nose. When Winston Aronson threw a snowball that took off the head of my snowman and sent the carrot flying, it was like a dagger to my heart.

Nancie, seeing my pain, bravely stood. Exposing herself to enemy fire, she threw a snowball across the street. It hit one of the Nazi-snowmen, sending its helmet into the street.

We cheered, buoyed by this victory.

After that, it was a massacre.

Snowmen fell on both sides. Pieces were scattered everywhere, across both yards. If they'd been able to bleed, the resulting carnage would surely have resembled a slaughterhouse. But even without blood it was a grizzly sight.

I'm proud to say my sisters and I gave as good as we got. Though outnumbered, we inflicted serious damage on the enemy camp.

This might have gone on forever, but late in the afternoon our father's car pulled into the driveway. The battle came to a halt. Dad, home from the hardware store he owned and ran, walked into the house with barely a glance in our direction. But this was our signal to go inside for supper.

After supper, during which Gloria, Nancie and I regaled our parents with a blow-by-blow description of our afternoon, it was dark and we had to stay in.

The next day being Sunday, we were kept busy all day with church, then visits to various relatives' houses. And, of course, on Monday there was school.

That week brought a warming trend that turned our snowmen, as well as our fort, to soggy mush. Any idea we might have had of rebuilding our army and resuming the battle melted away with Uncle Milty and the others.

In school later that week I was headed for the lunchroom when I saw Herb Aronson walking toward me in the hallway. He saw me at the same exact moment. Our eyes locked.

As we drew nearer to each other, I wondered what was about to transpire. My sisters and I had, in our opinion, kicked the Aronson siblings' butts. Would Herb exact his revenge here at school? I was tempted to take the coward's way out and duck into the girls' bathroom, but I couldn't do it. Whatever fate awaited me, I wouldn't meet it by cowering in a bathroom stall.

It seemed to me that Herb Aronson scowled as we drew closer. I gulped, and marched steadily forward.

Then, when we were nearly face-to-face, he veered and continued on by me without a word. But I saw the quick nod he gave as he went past, accompanied by a slight lifting of one corner of his mouth.

That nod, I knew, had been a salute of respect, from one soldier to another.

Margaret Fielding Roberts spent her childhood in Nebraska, where she learned to build the perfect snowman. She has passed that skill on to her grandchildren.

WALKING BEANS WASN'T SOMETHING YOU DID WITH YOUR DOG

A CUP OF CHILDHOOD

Theresa Link

"Can we *please* have a lemonade stand?" my daughter, Mollie, and her friend, Ashley, beg me in those mournful tones only five-year olds can truly master. Their faces are flushed pink from playing outside in the muggy afternoon heat.

As their pleas hang in the air, I run through in my mind all the reasons I don't want them to have a lemonade stand: *I'd* have to make the lemonade, *I'd* have to set up the stand, make the sign, sit and help them try to sell their lemonade, and finally, I didn't believe anyone would even stop to buy lemonade.

But their wide eyes, filled with simple hope, outweigh my objections. I finally agree, "Yes, I'll help you set up a lemonade stand."

Their excitement is contagious, and soon we're all having a good time making the lemonade, setting up the stand, and determining how much to charge for each glass. Like most five-year-olds, they have no concept of money, so they determine that we should charge "a nickel, a quarter, or whatever money they've got!"

I've become more relaxed by this point, and this sounds like a good plan to me, too.

We bring the pitcher of ice-cold lemonade out into the front yard and set it on the small red table where the girls are planning to make their fortune. They fill Dixie cups in preparation for their future customers.

Some of my grown-up worries creep in and I warn them not to fill too many cups. In the back of my mind, I fear they may not sell any.

The lemonade stand is set up and Mollie and Ashley are ready for the world. As I settle onto my lawn chair in the shade, I'm already thinking about how I'll try to make them feel better if their lemonade stand does turn out to be a failure.

But Mollie and Ashley are not prepared to fail. They begin hawking their lemonade like experienced carnivaliers: "Get your lemonade here! Fresh lemonade! Only costs a nickel, or a quarter, or whatever money you've got!" they yell to cars driving past, people walking their dogs, bicyclists out for an early evening ride, neighbors, anyone within earshot.

And then something incredible happens—their first customer. Our neighbor walks across the lawn to purchase a cup of lemonade.

Mollie and Ashley are thrilled! They give her a cup, take her money and thank her, and then watch with matching happy grins as their first customer enjoys her glass of lemonade.

No sooner does our neighbor finish her glass and return home than another neighbor appears, and then some neighbor children. People who appear to be on their way somewhere else—maybe to the grocery store, or home for dinner after a long day of work—pull their cars over to the side of the road, get out and buy lemonade. Some buy a glass, some buy several . . . and not a one of them pays only a nickel.

As I watch all this activity, I notice that not only are the kids having a wonderful time with their first taste of "business," but the adults who stop for a moment are also having a wonderful time enjoying their cup of childhood.

Everyone who comes to the lemonade stand does so with a smile and an open heart. They drink their lemonade as if they'd never before tasted such fine nectar. Some give business advice to the girls: "You need to charge much more than a nickel!"

Some are quiet as they drink their lemonade. Perhaps they're remembering their own childhoods. Maybe they're thinking about other hot, muggy evenings long ago, when they had a lemonade stand and they dreamed about all the possibilities open to them.

Everyone leaves feeling good.

The pitcher of lemonade empties. Most is sold, but some is spilled and some is enjoyed by Mollie and Ashley. I begin to feel a bit sad that all the fun is ending. I'd been enjoying sharing the good feelings around the lemonade stand.

I realize that my daughter and her friend have shared more than lemonade that evening. They shared a bit of common humanity. They gave people who may not even have been thirsty an opportunity to stop for just a moment, to savor a cup of lemonade, and to relive some nice memories from long ago.

Theresa Link has lived in a small Minnesota town for forty years. In her career she has the opportunity to travel all over the world, but having lived and raised her children in a small town, she is always happy to come home.

WALKING BEANS WASN'T SOMETHING YOU DID WITH YOUR DOG

ADVENTURES IN MUSHROOM HUNTING

Sherrie Bradford

Every year in Harrison County, Iowa, the Loess Hills turn from brown earthy hues to lush shades of green. If the transition from winter into spring was wet enough, and the temperature just right on these natural wind-blown hills, the Morel mushroom would grow.

Morels did not grow every spring. But when they did, my mother would get a phone call from our Uncle Leo. I remember those calls, and my mother saying with excitement, "Oh, yes, they'd love to help you out, Leo."

With those words, my three brothers and I knew not to plan anything for the next five days, give or take a day. We were being drafted to go mushroom hunting. If I were to say that I was excited and looked forward to searching for Morels, I'd be lying.

Mushroom hunting meant walking mile upon mile through the sandy-soiled hills, stooped over, looking for the elusive "grays" and the more rarely found "yellows," for the paltry fee of fifty cents an hour. Even in the late 1960s and early '70s, Uncle Leo was getting a bargain and possibly breaking several child labor laws in the process. If we'd known he was then selling Morels in brown paper bags for eight dollars a bag, we would have protested for higher wages.

Uncle Leo would arrive from his home in Omaha with netted onion bags for us to fill with mushrooms. He told us the netted bags were to allow the spores of the mushrooms to fall out as we carried the bags on our search in the hills.

This spread the spores, allowing more mushrooms to grow in the future. At least that was his theory, and I had no reason to doubt him.

The old pickup would arrive early the next day with Uncle Leo behind the steering wheel, beaming from ear to ear. He'd hand my brothers and me a bag and quip, "We'd better get out there while the pickin's good!"

I believe that Leo was a psychic when it came to hunting mushrooms. If there were any mushrooms in those hills to be found, he'd find them.

Morels come in all shapes and sizes, and anyone can hunt for them. They don't look anything like the poisonous toadstools or other wild-growing fungi. Their gray or yellowish cones appear spongy. That's why the dimpled heads must be cleaned well and soaked in salt water before preparing them to eat. The darker the head of the mushroom, the more pronounced and delicious its flavor.

The Morel mushroom is called the poor man's truffle. I don't know how a truffle tastes, as I've never had one. But I will say that Morels, when sliced, rolled in flour and seasonings, then fried in butter, are just about the best treat a taste bud can experience.

On the day of the hunt, we would all pile into the back of Leo's pickup, and he'd drive us to the first mushroom hunting spot of the season. Then we'd all pile out of the truck and follow Leo, carrying our netted bags.

The Loess Hills are beautiful. They rise majestically in Harrison County, and people come from all over the Midwest to see them. Most of the hills are also privately owned. Uncle Leo had a habit of not asking landowners if we could hunt for mushrooms on their property. To most people this was called trespassing. Leo called the Loess Hills "God's Country," insisting no one could own something this beautiful as created by God. Of course, the local authorities and landowners disagreed with him.

Each year, while hunting, we'd get at least one visit from a local authority, called by a landowner. The landowners might also ask us politely, and sometimes not so politely, to leave. There were those who would sic their dogs on us, and dogs that would sic themselves on us. We once encountered a man with a shotgun who told us that he used rice as buckshot.

I queried, "Really, how does that work?"

"Stick around and you'll find out," he answered.

Most of the time, however, landowners didn't know we were there, as we stayed far away from the houses.

We usually stayed together in groups of two and always had a designated meeting spot in case we were to become separated. Uncle Leo had us carry whistles around our necks to blow in case of an emergency. We used these most of the time when we were being chased by dogs. Uncle Leo carried doggy treats with him to deter the attention of the dogs when this happened.

Of course, doggy treats don't work with badgers. We were told to stay out of abandoned houses, but sometimes our curiosity outweighed the warning.

During one hunt, one of my brothers and I decided to explore a deserted, two-story house. As we entered through the door we were greeted by a pair of eyes and a snarl. It was a badger. I stood frozen, but my brother ran, urgently blowing his whistle. The badger chose to run right past me and instead go after the person who was annoying it the most.

Uncle Leo was right there with his walking stick in hand. He yelled, "I told you kids not to go into those old houses!"

My brother ran past Leo, with the badger hot on his heels. Leo raised his walking stick and whacked the badger several times before it darted off into the tall grass.

These were a few of the exciting and sometimes dangerous escapades we encountered while mushroom hunting in the Loess Hills. Most of the time the hunts were more mellow experiences. When the mushrooms were scarce, conversation was minimal. Mushroom hunting seemed like a lot of work during those times, and all I could think about was going home and doing anything other than looking for "grays" and "yellows."

But there were also times when we didn't have to search long and hard to find the Morels. At those times everyone would compare their bags to see who had found the most dimpled-headed mushrooms. The contests didn't stop there. We'd also check to see who had the largest or the most unusually-shaped mushroom.

Talking about school, activities, and friends helped to pass the time while stomping the hills. We would sing the songs that we learned in school, or that were on the "America's Top Forty" list that week. We often disagreed on the words of the popular songs of the time, which could result in an argument.

These were the times my brothers and I grew closer to each other, and to Uncle Leo. My brothers and I still like to reminisce about those hunts, nearly forty years later and long after Uncle Leo has passed away.

Now that I'm older, I have to admit I wouldn't have traded those days of hunting Morels for anything. Will I do it again? No, but not because I'm afraid of having the authorities called on me or of hard work. But rather because I've since moved and live in an area where they don't grow.

And I'm also somewhat nostalgic. Hunting for mushrooms would just never be the same without my brothers, Uncle Leo, and the fifty cents an hour.

Sherrie Bradford was born in South Texas, but her family returned to their Iowa roots when she was twelve years old. They lived in Missouri Valley, Iowa, in the heart of the Loess Hills, where her mother remains to this day.

Photo provided by Verla Klaessy

CHAUTAUQUA!

Verla Klaessy

Cherry stood by the Ionic columns bordering the porch of the mansion in which she worked. Across the street in the vacant block, a huge tent was being erected. On Grand Avenue it was cause for excitement, this summer in 1922 in the rural community. "Culture Under Canvas" was a bigger event than any circus or street carnival.

It was Chautauqua!

For seven days the stage under the tent would showcase the best in music, drama and even controversial social and political topics. Cherry hoped Mrs. Higgins, her employer, would allow her extra time to attend the events. Her daily job as housekeeper and cook for the family of the mansion took most of her time, but she could hardly contain her emotions as she anticipated all the entertainment and learning that would be going on just across the street from where she lived and worked.

Banners and posters decorated the town, proclaiming the best in good clean instructive entertainment, as well as the chance to learn about the world outside their hometown.

While cleaning, Cherry overheard a discussion in the library that Mr. Higgins had with his lawyer friend about the origins of the name Chautauqua. The name, she learned, was borrowed from the Lyceum located on Lake Chautauqua in New York at the Chautauqua Institute. That was where social and political events of the day were discussed regularly by some of the best thinkers in the country.

Mr. Higgins and his friend talked about orators expounding on such subjects as, "Have we learned how to make a living, but not a life?" "Do we have more knowledge, but less judgment?" "More experts, yet more problems?"

As Cherry listened behind the pocket doors, she marveled at people sharing such thoughts and ideas with one another. Her own schooling had been cut short when she'd had scarlet fever in the eighth grade and she'd never returned to school. Yet her thirst for learning had never left her, and she didn't feel it was a bad thing to eavesdrop this time.

Though Cherry had learned to play the piano from her Aunt Rosie, she knew she'd never be a successful musician. But she loved listening to music and knew it was one of the important parts of the Chautauqua circuit. To satisfy a wide range of musical tastes, everything from full choirs to marching bands, opera singers, bell ringers and even Swiss yodelers would perform.

Chautauqua stage offered drama and poetry readings, Shakespeare plays as well as magicians and the wise-cracking of Charlie McCarthy, the ventriloquist's dummy. Something for all ages was included.

Much of the program was entertainment, but it also featured inspirational speakers such as judges, congressmen, and even United States presidents. The speakers kept the audience cheering, laughing and sometimes even crying. The famous golden voice of William Jennings Bryan stirred the crowd, and his speeches were often repeated. Teddy Roosevelt was a popular speaker and called Chautauqua "the most American thing in America!"

Timidly, Cherry approached her employer about attending more than one performance, as it was just across the street. Mrs. Higgins thought about it, and decided if Cherry could maintain her work schedule, perhaps by arising an hour earlier in the mornings, she would be allowed to observe more than one night's program.

The steady stream of carriages and motor cars coming and going to the event across the street made for a lively scene. Stylish ladies in the latest frocks, accompanied by gentlemen in top hats, sat in wooden folding chairs in the front rows. Behind them were the rows of wooden slat benches for those not quite as high up on the social ladder, and dressed in less fancy attire. Farm folks in their best Sunday outfits, little girls with big ribbons in their hair and young lads with their hair slicked down filled the remainder of the tent. On very warm nights the sides of the tent were rolled up to let in the breezes.

Cherry watched the spectacle across the street as often as she could, wishing she could join the throng. After the second night, Mr. Higgins handed her a ticket and told her to go and enjoy herself. She was thrilled to have an extra night off, as well as to be allowed to see for herself all the wonderful things she'd so far only imagined.

It was even better than she had dreamed. A marching band in blue and gold uniforms marched down the aisle and onto the stage, playing "The Star Spangled Banner." Three tumblers in black tights did amazing maneuvers as they climbed onto each other's shoulders and then tossed each other back and forth. A buxom lady sang an aria from an opera, her voice reaching the highest notes Cherry had ever heard.

Cherry was swept away by a poem that brought tears to her eyes, and laughed heartily at a clown trying to climb a ladder. She listened intently to a speaker who told of the terrible conditions in the slums in the big cities and how workers were needed to help clear the areas of the plague of poverty. His words touched Cherry's heart so much that she resolved to someday make that her life's work.

Later in the week, on her regular night off, Cherry's boyfriend took her to the Chautauqua again. After the introduction, and a performance by a seven-member girls' band, a young girl played the marimba. When she finished, the applause was thunderous. Then the crowd laughed uproariously as a man in a tub went through all kinds of antics as he pretended to bathe.

Solos and readings were followed by another orator expounding on, "What Shall You Do With Your Leisure?" Cherry thought that leisure was only for those who could hire someone to do their work.

Later, as she lay in her bed in her attic room, Cherry relived every moment of the wonderful events she'd experienced at the Chautauqua.

The world out there was even bigger than she had imagined.

Verla Klaessy lives in Spencer, Iowa, and often writes about her mother, Cherry Brewer, who worked for a time as a maid in the historic Higgins Mansion.

GOING TO THE FAIR

Janet Branson

Don't you just love going to the fair? I do. As a child I remember going to the big regional fair every summer. We got up early and quickly did the chores. While we finished that, Mom would fix a nice lunch to take along.

It was all so exciting. There were so many things to do and see, we hardly knew where to start. I liked to go with my mother and see all the canned goods and handiwork that ladies had brought in. We always looked at the tags to see if we knew any of the names. Sometimes we'd notice a blue ribbon that one of my mother's friends had received on her canned goods.

One summer someone came to our farm and asked if we'd like to enter a sheaf of our own wheat in the fair, so we did. I don't remember if we won a ribbon for that sheaf, but it was exciting to go to the fair and look for it. Our sheaf had been tied up in a special way, and we all agreed it looked very pretty.

Daddy and the boys, of course, went to look at all the new farm machinery.

Once I saw something at the fair that I've never forgotten. One of the feed dealers had eggs with green, red and orange yolks. My mother didn't like them. She said they looked awful. I, of course, being a kid, thought they were pretty impressive.

After an hour or so with our parents, my brother Jerry and I could go off by ourselves and do whatever we wanted, and that was to head out for the Midway to ride the rides.

Daddy always gave us two dollars. We could go on a lot of rides with that money.

As a teenager, one of my favorite rides was called The Roundup. On The Roundup you entered a round cylinder and stood against the wall. The cylinder began to spin around faster and faster, and then the floor dropped out but you stuck to the wall as the centrifugal force held you there. It was so much fun, I wanted to go again and again!

Another thing that I loved was something called Dancing Waters, which was a water and light show controlled by what reminded me of an organ console. Water sprayed out of the jets to orchestrated music and colored lights shone in the water—truly beautiful to watch.

One year my brother Jerry and I cooked up a scheme. I suppose I was about twelve and he was ten. We had seen all those games in the Midway and had decided not to go on any rides that year, but to spend our money to win something. Of course, we didn't tell our parents.

We were so excited at the thought of winning some prizes, we could hardly wait. After eating lunch at the car, and taking our two dollars plus a little extra saved from our allowances, we made our way to the Midway.

The men in those booths called to us and made it sound like so much fun. There were many cute toys to win. I remember one place had strings tied together in a bunch. The player pulled on a string, and whatever was tied to the end of it was the prize. We were going to try it! We gave the man our quarter and pulled a string.

Nothing but a piece of bubble gum for our quarter.

"Well," said the man, "why don't you try it again? Maybe this time you'll be lucky."

We plunked down another quarter. This time we surely would be lucky. We chose another string and pulled on it. Another piece of gum. Disappointed, we left that game and looked for something else. We tried throwing a ball to knock over some pins, but couldn't do that either. Every game we tried, we lost. In the end we spent all of our money trying to win a fun prize, and all we had to show for our efforts were a few pieces of bubble gum.

It was going to be two or three more hours before it was time to meet our parents and go home. That was a very long time with no money. Jerry and I walked around the fairgrounds, looked at the rides and the food places, but all of our money was gone.

Finally, it was time to meet our parents.

"Hi, kids," they said. "Did you have fun on all the rides?"

We hung our heads.

"What's the matter, didn't you have any fun?"

"No."

"Oh, you didn't? Why is that?"

"We spent all our money to win some toys and didn't even win anything."

"Oh, really? That's too bad. Do you think you learned a lesson from it?"

We nodded our heads. They didn't scold us. We'd learned our lesson. In later years we were able to laugh about it, but that was the last time I was ever tempted to gamble away my money.

Janet Branson and her husband, Pastor Bruce Branson, live in Hartley, Iowa. She's the mother of five grown sons and has ten beautiful grandchildren. Besides writing, she enjoys genealogy and refurbishing antique furniture.

WALKING BEANS WASN'T SOMETHING YOU DID WITH YOUR DOG

WATERFALL DREAMS

Heather Patterson

It was the promise of swimming in waterfalls that got me out of bed that morning. Normally a seven-year old rises early during the summer months only for cartoons, but I loved our trips to Starved Rock State Park. This day would be no exception.

The sky was bright blue with a few wispy clouds as we packed a picnic basket for lunch and a backpack of other necessities for a day of hiking. With my arms and legs plastered with bug spray and sunblock, I piled into the backseat of our Jeep Golden Eagle. My older brother by two years situated himself beside me, and our parents climbed into the front seats. They had removed the soft top, as well as the doors, leaving us completely exposed to the elements. Our only protection was the padded rollbar—and Dad's driving skills.

We were not long into our half-hour journey before my brother and I decided we were hungry. After much begging on our part, Mom told us to grab a snack from the bag behind us. The wind whipped through our hair and the morning sun beat down on our faces as we munched on Keebler Townhouse crackers and dreamed of what the day would hold for us.

The drive there was an adventure in itself. The back roads of LaSalle County were, on occasion, twisty and hilly.

One road in particular was our favorite. Our youthful, creative minds had labeled it "The Hilly Road," and my brother and I had perfected the method of riding it. We'd inhale as the vehicle rose up the hill, and as it went down the other side we held our breath and felt our stomachs rise. It had the same effect as a mild roller coaster. The steeper the descent, the better the feeling. We rose and fell, gasping for breath, our giggles filling the air.

The landscape along the way was breathtaking, as well. Miles and miles of cornfields and prairie land flew past, interrupted every now and then by a house or a small town. Tall, wild grasses and flowers along the ditches swayed in the breeze, and the sun glinted off large puddles in fields from a recent rain. Dreams emerged of hidden cottages and adventures with animals in the scattered woodlands throughout the flowing plains . . . a real-life Narnia.

We watched for landmarks along the way, and there was one particular landmark we always eagerly anticipated: the Slugbug Farm. It was a burial ground (read "junkyard") for old slugbugs—slang for Volkswagen Beetles. They were in all conditions, from "slightly rusty" to "Swiss cheese," and dotted the property liberally, springing from the weeds like clusters of brightly colored flowers.

So popular were slugbugs that a game evolved from their creation: the Slugbug Game (or Punch Buggy as known in other areas).

It was quite popular with bored children on the road, and has a similar concept as the Pididdle Game (which is to locate a vehicle with one burned out headlight), except you played Slugbug in daylight.

The rules, as we knew them, were to be the first to call out the proper name, depending on its color, and rack up the most points. My goal was always to avoid the consequence of being too slow to speak up, which was to be punched in the arm.

The only prize was to walk away with the fewest bruises. The Slugbug Farm was the jackpot when it came to this game.

As the Jeep rounded a corner, I scooted as far forward in my seat as the seatbelt would allow. My eyes searched the horizon for the first glimpse of hot sun reflecting off shiny orbs beyond the fence that surrounded the property. Specifically, I was looking for red roofs—known as Beaver-Cleavers—which were worth five points, whereas all of the other slugbug colors—known as Jack-Knifes—were worth only one point each.

My mouth opened, but my brother shouted, "Beaver-Cleaver!" first and awarded me with a punch to the upper right arm. A war ensued to see who could call out more names than the other as we counted on our fingers and doled out the punches.

The Jeep approached and passed the farm. First our necks and then our bodies turned as we kept calling out "Jack-knife!" and pointing to the cars, our fingers curling and uncurling, counting to five . . . ten . . . fifteen.

As the farm disappeared behind us and we untangled ourselves from the harnesses that had kept us from falling out of the open-sided vehicle, our parents looked back at us and rolled their eyes. With a strong punch to my right shoulder, my brother said, "I win," and we settled back to observing the landscape.

Having been in the sun for a half-hour already, the thought of cooling off in freshwater pools made me shiver with excitement.

Dad pulled the Jeep off the road into a small, gravel parking lot, and we unloaded the vehicle. As Mom surveyed the lunch contents, she discovered that my brother and I had eaten most of the crackers. We received a scolding, and then everyone grabbed his or her fanny-pack and handmade walking sticks.

It was much cooler here, below the canopy of trees. The sounds from unseen animals echoed around us, distorting the location of their true source. Leaves rustled above from startled birds, and cicadas started a symphony in stereo, soon joined by other insects. Or had they been there all along?

Our path eventually led us to an overlook, where we saw the Illinois River below us. Dad said we could go closer, so we left the traditional path and carefully maneuvered down to a sandy inlet. The water was green and brown, and algae and other debris bobbed on the surface as the water rolled in and out. We skipped rocks, drew designs in the sand with the tips of our walking sticks, and investigated the shallow caves in the rock walls before Dad said we needed to keep moving if we wanted to get to the waterfall.

We needed no further urging.

Back up on the trail, we hiked for a while longer before my brother and I complained of the heat and sore feet and empty bellies. We backtracked to a point to rest on a bench with Mom while Dad went back to the Jeep to retrieve the picnic basket. When he returned, we followed another path deeper into the forest.

The sun peeked through the lace-like green foliage above us. Our breathing grew deeper and slower, and the terrain became rougher.

There were areas where we had to walk single-file around tree roots jutting from the ground, maneuver up and down sharp slopes embedded with jagged rocks, climb over large limbs that had fallen across the path, and avoid slipping on muddy spots that the sun had not reached to dry.

We batted away nosey bugs that were ignorant of the careful tactics we had undergone that morning to prevent contact with them, and more than once I wondered why we were doing this.

Eventually we came to a point where we left the main trail and could hear rushing water in the distance. My heart sped up at the thought of how close we were. Our spirits lightened and we hurried ahead, brushing away spindly tree branches and ducking under low-hanging limbs. The sound of water grew even closer, and then I was gazing upon the prize I'd sought all morning.

Hundreds of feet above us, water gushed between rock formations and crashed down to a floor of St. Peter sandstone, carving a series of large, natural stair-steps. The water gathered in large pools on each level before spilling farther down into the forest.

We weren't alone. Scattered about on the flat, rocky areas around the pools were other families who'd had the same idea as ours. We claimed our spot, spread out a blanket, and dug into the cooler.

As far as experiences go, lunch beside a waterfall in the forest is a truly amazing thing.

Once our bellies were full, my brother and I quickly discarded our clothes to reveal our swimwear beneath. We carefully made our way toward the pools and slipped into the clear water. Though bitterly cold, it was a refreshing change from the heat we'd experienced during our hike, even with the cover of leaves.

The depth of most of the pools was only waist-high on a child sitting down. Other pools farther down were deep enough to reach almost chest-high, but they were harder to get to. The laughter and splashing of children echoed against the rocky walls, rising above the sounds of nature that the adults were trying to enjoy.

All too soon, it was time to leave. We dried off and packed up our things—careful not to leave any trash behind—and made our way back to the trail.

I was full and tired from the hike and the swim, which made the return walk back seem longer. There were more pauses for breaks than there had been on the way to the waterfall, and the trek was harder since we were now going uphill.

But the trees eventually released us and we stepped out onto the parking lot.

The gravel of the parking lot covered my wet and muddy shoes in a coat of gray dust. I got back into the Jeep and nestled in my seat behind Dad. Wrapped up in my towel, I leaned my head against the padding of the rollbar beside me.

As we pulled out onto the highway, I stared at the sun that had moved across the sky. It had been a long day, but well worth the trip to swim in LaSalle Canyon Falls. I yawned and closed my eyes, not caring that my brother would win at the Slugbug Game on the way home, or that I would probably wake up with aching muscles from the hike.

As I look back, I'm glad I have these memories of our family outings. Especially the hikes, where we ventured off the main trails to hidden places in the forests.

I never found magical cottages or fairy animals, but swimming in crystalline waterfalls and picnic lunches under a green canopy were a far greater pleasure.

You can't leave the marked trails at Starved Rock anymore. That's unfortunate. I know it's for the hikers' safety, but there's a world out there that's still unseen by human eyes.

I guess that's what dreams are for.

Heather Patterson is a freelance writer who lives in Central Illinois with her cat, Daisy Mae. In her free time she enjoys dancing, watching movies and playing with her niece.

HIGH SCHOOL DAYS
IN A SMALL IOWA TOWN

Ruth Jochims

I was fifteen years old when I timidly left my home in Des Moines to attend a Seventh-Day Adventist boarding school in Nevada, Iowa.

I was excited and apprehensive as I sat in the back seat with my sisters during the drive there. I didn't know who my roommate would be, and that was a little scary. I was shy, and I know my parents thought this experience would be good for me.

My older sister had already graduated from the boarding school. She knew how I felt, and tried to encourage me. I cried a little, but dried my tears as the car chugged up the hill to Oak Park Academy.

After registering, we carried boxes of my belongings up to the third floor, where I met my friendly roommate, Ginny. I got settled in, and my family left.

Though I missed my family, I soon adjusted to dorm life and made friends.

Our days at the academy began early, with worship in the girls' and boys' dorms. Attendance was taken and we were expected to be there, or we'd better have a good excuse.

After worship was breakfast, then classes, and chapel at 10:00 a.m.

Those students with musical ability played the piano and organ for the religious services. Jackie, a good friend of mine, was very talented. She played the piano and organ, and during special times was allowed to play peppier songs. Sometimes she'd have me turn the pages for her as she played. I had taken piano and organ lessons, too, and by my junior year I also was playing during the religious services.

After dinner, we all had jobs to do to help pay our tuition. I worked in the kitchen my freshman year. During the following years I worked at the switchboard and then the laundry.

I also worked as a night watchman. That was a little scary, because I had to patrol the dark halls with a flashlight every hour, checking that no one was trying to leave or break in. I could study in between times, but this wasn't a good job for me. I was supposed to go to bed early so I could get up at 2:00 a.m. to begin my shift.

Often I had trouble getting to sleep because my roommate would still be awake, and with the light on. I wasn't a good sleeper anyway, and my heart pounded with worry until I finally had to tell the Dean that I couldn't do the job any more. She was understanding, and found someone else to take my place.

There were other jobs for the students. There was work in the print shop, in a broom shop, and there was dairy and other farm work. These were good jobs for the boys, though girls also worked in the broom shop and print shop.

Sometimes at night we'd come out of our rooms to goof off during study time. The Dean had an eagle eye, and if we were caught we were likely to be punished. I overheard some girls talking about having to shovel "sunshine" (manure) as punishment.

Late one night my roommate and I were awakened by a knock at our door. It was the Dean. She told us to quickly put on our shoes and robes and follow her.

When we got outside, we saw fire coming out of one of the third floor windows. Soon, fire trucks arrived.

My roommate and I found it exciting to watch the firemen fighting the flames, which were confined to an empty room. The fire was soon put out, and we were allowed to go back to our rooms.

How did the fire start? We later learned that two girls had been smoking, and had put their stubs out in the window casing. The penalty for the girls was dismissal from school for two weeks, and when they came back they remained on probation.

We had some good times at school. After supper we could go to the gymnasium and watch the boys play basketball. On other nights we roller-skated to recorded music, and the boys sometimes asked the girls to skate with them.

One day a week we could sign out and go to town, which was within walking distance. We were warned to never get caught in a place called the Candy Kitchen. Liquor was sold there, and it had a bad reputation.

I auditioned for a choir, and was thrilled when I was accepted. Our choir group traveled to many Seventh-Day Adventist churches throughout Iowa and Minnesota. One of the churches we traveled to was in Spencer, Iowa. I never dreamed I would live there some day.

Sometimes, for a treat, the students and teachers would walk to a drive-in restaurant on the other side of town. It was there that I discovered the joys of French fries and malts. These were special treats for me, as my family never went out to eat. It was always Mom's home cooking for us.

Each year at school we had a banquet with a special theme. The girls wore formals, and could go with a guy if she were lucky enough to be asked. Those girls who didn't have dates went together in groups and had just as good a time. After the banquet, a movie would be shown.

One year the banquet had an Oriental theme. By this time my younger sister, Doris, was also attending the academy. My mother found us some Oriental-looking robes and slippers. We looked the part for the banquet, but I never did master the chopsticks.

Every year the academy also had a talent show. Once I played in a piano quartet, and we won third prize. Another year Doris and I played a piano duet.

Every six weeks during the school year, and on holidays, I went home for a short vacation. It was always nice to be home, but by then I missed my friends. And Des Moines was so different from the small town of Nevada that I'd become accustomed to.

One school year the Asian flu hit us so hard that the school was closed down for a week. Miserable and sick, I rode home with some other students from Des Moines. I wanted my own bed and my mom's tender loving care.

My senior year was a year of parties and picture taking. For our senior trip, our class went to Kansas City. Any student wanting to go had to have at least a "C" in all subjects. I was a little worried about my poor grades, but I buckled down and surprised myself by getting high enough grades to go.

One of my teachers told me she was proud of me, and that she'd known I could do it.

I have many fond memories of my home-away-from-home during those school years. I've been told that I led a sheltered life. Perhaps I did, but I like to think my time at the academy prepared me for life's hardships.

Ruth Jochims lives in Spencer, Iowa with her husband, Victor. She belongs to two writing groups and especially enjoys writing poetry.

WATCHING *BONANZA*
ON COLOR TELEVISION

J. N. Curtis

In 1962 our family had a little black and white television set in our living room. It served us well for many years. Every chance I had, I would lie on my belly two feet in front of it, my chin propped on my hands, captivated by the flickering images on the screen.

My favorite program back then was *Bonanza*. Each week I waited eagerly for Sunday night to roll around. In my opinion, *Bonanza* was the most important thing about Sunday evenings. My parents had other ideas about what was important. Supper, for instance. As fixed by my mother, supper was a serious meal that always consisted of meat, potatoes and gravy, biscuits with butter, and vegetables. She believed in feeding my dad and me well, and hurrying through a meal was not an option. I was expected to clean my plate before I'd be excused from the table.

Sometimes, getting released from the table wasn't dependent only on my stuffing myself to my mother's satisfaction. My father could hold things up, as well. A born storyteller, he liked nothing more than a captive audience.

". . . then Mrs. Sundhagen came into the office, and she had the biggest boil on her rear I've ever seen on a human being," he told us one Sunday evening, leaning back in his chair and drumming his fingers on his chest.

"John, that's not proper talk for the table," my mother scolded.

My father was the doctor in our small town. He had an office on Main Street, but he might well be called out to visit someone's home if they needed him. He was sometimes even asked to take a look at some farmer's prize cow, or a mare that was about to foal. The nearest veterinarian was sixty miles away.

Sometimes I went with him on his house calls. My father was determined that I would also be a doctor. I was just as determined that I would be anything but a doctor. Cowboy was one possibility I was considering.

On that particular evening, I had just been released from the table when the phone rang. It was Mr. Norheim, calling my dad to ask him to come out to his farm because Mrs. Norheim was "feeling poorly." The Norheims lived a few miles outside of town, so Dad tried to convince the farmer to bring his wife to the office in the morning. Mr. Norheim insisted she wasn't well enough to make the trip.

My dad told me to come along, and soon we were heading for the Norheim farm on bumpy back roads, across a wooden bridge that creaked under the weight of our old station wagon, and around a cow that had gotten past its fence and wasn't ready to give up its place in the center of the road.

When we finally reached the Norheim farm, I could tell my dad was out of sorts. He'd been mostly silent during the trip. Usually, when I went with him on these calls, he would use the opportunity to tell me stories about his time as a medic during WWII. He had hundreds of stories. So many, in fact, that I sometimes wondered how he'd managed to squeeze so many adventures into a two-year stint in the military.

But, even though he was less than happy about this long trip out to the country, my father gave no indication of that when he got out of the car to greet Mr. Norheim. He wore only his usual smile as he carried his black medical bag to the front porch.

"'Evening," my father said. "Let's take a look at your wife."

I trailed behind, feeling grumpy because I didn't want to be there. So I didn't see my dad's face when Mr. Norheim said, "Tell ya da truth, Doc, it's not da missus I called ya out here for. It's for Jezebel."

My father stopped so abruptly that I walked smack into his back. He said, "Mr. Norheim . . . "

"Now, I knew ya wouldn't drive all da way out here ta see Jezebel," the farmer cut in.

"You were right about that," my father agreed.

Mrs. Norheim stepped out onto the porch. "I told him not to tell you dat lie, Doctor, but he's stubborn an' he never listens to me." She had the same thick Norwegian accent as her husband. In her fifties, and a couple of decades younger than her husband, Mrs. Norheim was an imposing figure of a woman. Taller than my father, who topped six feet, she towered over her diminutive husband. She wore an apron over her housedress, and her legs were as broad and sturdy as two oak trunks. She didn't look as though she'd been sick a day in her life. She certainly wasn't ailing at this time.

Jezebel, the patient my father had been duped into seeing, was Mr. Norheim's blue-ribbon sow, which had taken honors at the county fair three years running.

"Mr. Norheim," my father said in a low voice. "It's Sunday, and I like to spend this time with my family."

"Well, I can 'preciate that," the farmer said. "And I see ya brought your fine young man with ya." He nodded genially at me.

My father sighed. "As long as I'm here, I might as well take a look at Jez."

I fully expected to go to the barn with my father. But, before we could head in that direction, Mrs. Norheim spoke again. "Maybe da young man would rather come inside here and watch television with me." Then she let loose with the clincher. "We have da color television."

I nearly swooned. I'd caught glimpses of color television in store windows, but hadn't had the opportunity to sit and watch an entire episode of any program on one. And it was just about time for my all-time favorite program to start.

I looked at my father with naked hope. His previously stern expression softened. He knew what this meant to me. "Go on," he said with a tilt of his chin.

I scrambled up the front steps of the Norheim home while my father and the farmer headed for the barn.

Mrs. Norheim led me to the front parlor, where their television set rested. She told me it was a "console" as she reached down to turn it on. Then, saying she was going to get some cookies for me, she left me alone in the parlor.

I sat on the floor in front of the television set. There was little about the Norheims to suggest they would spring for such a luxury item, but I knew looks could be deceiving. The outside of their house, as well as the barn and outbuildings, were in need of paint and repair, and I'd heard my father complain that getting Farmer Norheim to pay his bills was like trying to take a soup bone from a dog. Yet Mr. Norheim drove a shiny Ford pickup, and his wife drove a Cadillac with fins big enough to swath through a field of hay, if she were so inclined. And I'd caught a glimpse into their kitchen on my way to the parlor. In it I'd seen what looked like a brand new refrigerator. It sure didn't look anything like the old Frigidaire in our kitchen at home, the one Mom had to regularly chip at the interior of with a butter knife.

But I wasn't there to worry about Mr. Norheim paying or not paying his medical bills. I was going to watch *Bonanza* on color television.

It turned out to be everything I'd imagined. The show had just begun when Mrs. Norheim returned with a plate of cookies and a glass of milk.

"Here ya go, young man," she said cheerfully.

With my eyes riveted on Ben, Adam, Hoss and Little Joe in living color, I took the plate and glass of milk she offered. I did manage to murmur, "Thank you, ma'am."

Little Joe had just drawn his gun and was peering around the corner of a barn, taking aim at some bad guys. The barn was red! The sky overhead was blue! Little Joe's eyes were hazel!

I took a bite of cookie, my mind barely registering that it was oatmeal raisin and I hated oatmeal raisin cookies. Mrs. Norheim could have fed me ground glass and I wouldn't have noticed. Hoss was getting on his horse, ready to pursue the bad guys Little Joe had just chased off the Ponderosa. Hoss's eyes were blue, and the poor horse seemed to sag under his weight.

It was nearing the end of the episode and we were watching a Chevrolet commercial when my father appeared in the doorway.

"Time to go, Butch," he said. I was stricken, and it must have shown on my face because my father leaned on the doorframe and added, "I guess we can stay for a couple of more minutes."

On the drive home I gave my father a detailed recap of the *Bonanza* episode, how amazing, more alive everything had looked in living color. "Can we get a color television, Dad?" I begged as we pulled into the driveway of our home.

My father grunted. "As long as patients like Norheim expect me to treat them and their livestock for free, I don't see it in our future, son."

"What was wrong with Jez?" I asked.

"Probably colic," he said, "but I'll keep an eye on her for the next few days."

And therein lay my father's credo as a doctor. He knew he was unlikely to be paid by Mr. Norheim, yet, having taken on the responsibility of Jezebel's care, he wouldn't turn his back on her.

And my father did continue to treat Jezebel, whose condition turned out to be more serious than at first believed. She pulled through, thanks in large part to his efforts, and would go on to win more blue ribbons in her long and distinguished life.

I went along with my father to every visit to the Norheims' that I could. Mrs. Norheim always invited me inside to watch the color television, and I would leave an hour or so later, dazed by the beauty of it all.

After Jezebel was on the mend, I heard my father on the phone with Mr. Norheim several times. They were discussing my father's fee. That much was obvious, and it was also obvious that Norheim, though grateful Jezebel would recover, was characteristically reluctant to part with any cash for my father's services.

Then, one day about a month after our last visit to the Norheim farm, my father called out to me as I was hanging upside down on my tire swing in the backyard, "C'mon, Butch, we're going for a ride."

I dropped from the tire and headed for our car.

"Not that way," my father said. "We're taking Uncle Pete's pickup."

My Uncle Pete's gunmetal gray International Harvester was parked across the street, with Uncle Pete behind the steering wheel. "Hiya, Butchy," he greeted me as Dad and I approached.

"Where are we going?" I asked as I climbed into the back of the pickup, where I always rode.

"You'll see," my dad said. He got in the front, next to Uncle Pete.

My curiosity was aroused, especially when we left town and started down the gravel roads. We were taking the route to the Norheim place, but, since I knew Jezebel was better, I didn't know why we would be going there.

A few minutes later we did, indeed, pull up to the Norheim farm. Mr. and Mrs. Norheim were both on the front porch. They appeared to be expecting us.

When I scrambled down from the back of the pickup, my father said, "You wait here."

My father and Uncle Pete went into the house with Mr. and Mrs. Norheim.

I was in torment! What were they doing in there? After a couple of minutes Mrs. Norheim came back out with a glass of milk and a plate of cookies for me.

Oatmeal raisin.

"I know how ya love my cookies," she said, beaming at me.

I managed to choke down a couple of cookies with the help of the milk. I was dying to ask Mrs. Norheim what the men were doing inside, but I knew my father wouldn't approve of my questioning her, so I remained silent.

It didn't take long for the mystery to be solved. Mr. Norheim appeared and held open the front door while my father and Uncle Pete came out, carrying the console color television set between them.

They brought the television to the pickup and set it in the back.

I looked at Mr. and Mrs. Norheim. They were both smiling, so I knew this was not some type of larceny taking place. Mr. Norheim even came over to me and put a hand on my shoulder. "You enjoy da stories now, young fella," he said.

All during the ride home I kept one hand protectively on the television to keep it from getting jostled. When we got back to our house, Uncle Pete backed the pickup into our driveway.

This was too good to be true!

Dad and Uncle Pete unloaded the television from the rear of the pickup. This time it was my mother who held the door open for them. At last I had the opportunity to ask some questions.

"Mr. Norheim decided that rather than pay me cash to settle his account, he'd prefer to give me something else of value," Dad told me as he and Uncle Pete situated the television in our front room. "They knew how much you enjoyed watching color television, so we agreed this would be a good trade."

Was it ever! I was in heaven.

We were the first family on our block to have color television, and I became something of a celebrity at school. I was soon watching other television shows in color as well. *The Jetsons, Mr. Ed* and *The Andy Griffith Show* were a few of my favorites.

The tradeoff, as I learned not long after the television arrived at our home, hadn't been quite the evenly matched deal I'd at first assumed. My mother filled me in on the details. Though Mr. Norhiem had owed my father a fair amount for his medical services, it hadn't equaled the value of the television. So my father had agreed to, in addition, treat Mr. and Mrs. Norheim's various medical needs for a year for free.

They may have taken advantage of the situation. Though my father didn't complain, I know that over the course of the next year they saw him for everything from Mrs. Norheim's "vapors" to a splinter in Mr. Norheim's thumb—a condition the farmer surely would have previously taken care of himself.

None of us regretted the deal that had been made. I continued to watch *Bonanza* and my other programs.

My mother liked *Ben Casey* and was delighted when her afternoon stories converted to color a couple of years later. My father, a sports fan, watched football in color. And I saw the moon landing from the sofa in our living room with my first girlfriend, slipping my arm across her shoulders as she sat mesmerized by the events on the screen.

That RCA color television set stayed with my family for another twenty years. Back then, things were built to last.

And *Bonanza* was cancelled the year I started medical school.

J. N. Curtis, M.D. practiced medicine in Wisconsin, Illinois and Indiana. He still watches reruns of *Bonanza* every chance he gets.

Photo provided by Loren Gaylord Flaugh

THE BEST OF TIMES

Loren Gaylord Flaugh

With my military service and a brief stint in Vietnam behind me, 1969 became a seemingly endless summer of fun and frolic. With beer parties and other reckless adventures, some stupid, to test my nerve, life was care-free. At twenty-one years of age, one doesn't always take things seriously.

Life was a breeze now that I had a sit-down job driving semi and hauling livestock hither and yon. When Robert Van Beek, a high school classmate and someone who helped me get through advanced algebra, proposed an intriguing idea, I couldn't say no.

"I have an old '55 Chevy that's ready for the junkyard. There's going to be a demolition derby at the O'Brien County Fair in a couple of weeks. If Grothaus and I prepare the car, do you want to drive it?" Van Beek asked.

Ron Grothaus was another classmate and drinking buddy. Grothaus and Van Beek worked for Lenz Manufacturing in Paullina during the summer when they were home from college. Both were skilled welders, with Grothaus being the better of the two. Robert's idea sounded like fun. "Yeah, I'll drive the car," I replied. What could go wrong?

With great gusto we began preparing the car, which involved bashing in the windows with heavy sledgehammers. Grothaus's moneymaking idea was to weld the trunk and the door seams shut. Two thirds of the car became a formidable battering ram. Nothing would yield until the very end, if at all.

The exciting event was set for the opening night of the fair on Monday, July 20. As more than a thousand excited fans filled the bleachers, seventeen other drivers entered the popular event, which meant three "heats" of six cars each. To be sure, this promised to make for a raucous evening.

Mankind was on the verge of journeying to the moon and leaving his first tentative footsteps on the lunar surface. "One small step for man, one giant leap for mankind," as Neil Armstrong said. On the other hand, I was about to have the time of my life.

Six cars in two rows lined up face-to-face. Two basic safety rules were explained at the drivers' meeting. Using the front end of your car to bash another car was a no-no. Smashing a car into another driver's door was the other no-no. When the judge signaled us to have at each other, the noise from loud mufflers, bedlam, chaos and carnage instantly erupted.

Driving the Chevy, I dashed for an open spot, turned it around and aimed for the arena's center. After I'd sustained a neck-jerking crash or two, I gleefully realized that this was even more fun than I'd thought it would be. It was wild! Was this my life's calling?

Chaos reigned supreme for ten minutes as I meted out punishment to many cars, though I took many hard licks, too. As a bumblebee would flitter and flutter about from one flower to the next, I delivered many stinging blows with the rear end of my car. My quickness seemed to be an advantage.

Near the race's end, the Chevy blew a radiator hose, sending out a geyser of steam from beneath the hood. Simply put, I'd struck a gusher. Somehow I managed to keep Old Faithful's hot engine running. The body damage to my car was inconsequential as compared to the others, and I was the last vehicle moving. I was declared the winner and was already eager for the next race.

My pit crew readied the car for the next event. A crude patch job fixed the radiator, and Grothaus's welding job had taken the punishment well. Indeed, his unibody design had made all the difference. Other cars had their rear ends either plowing a furrow, or bent straight up behind the axle.

Five other drivers and I drove out for the championship heat. We lined up in the muddy, mucky middle and waited for the melee to commence. But something soon broke in the clutch linkage. My car's body was in great shape, but alas, I couldn't budge and was now a sitting duck.

No more flitting about for me.

The gears began grinding inside my head. I was thinking hard. What could I do to get moving? By placing my right foot against the shifter handle and pushing hard, I found I could grind the car into reverse without stalling the engine. And by gripping the handle with both hands and pulling back, I could grind the car into low gear. I was back in business, sort of. Who needs a clutch, anyway? I'd created a new form of automatic transmission.

The crowd went wild at my hilarious mode of operation, for they could clearly hear me grinding gears every time I changed direction. It must have sounded like an Elliot Ness Tommy-gun firing at Al Capone. I knocked out a couple of cars until only one other driver, Jon Spang Jr., remained. Spang and I played cat and mouse amongst the wreckage that littered the arena. But I was one mighty crippled mouse.

With my useless clutch, I wasn't nearly fast enough to avoid Spang, as he brutally, repeatedly, bashed my car. When all was done my car was the vanquished, Spang's the victorious. True, I had only second place, but did I ever have a ball! I'd never had more fun in my life.

I felt the effects of my adventure over the next few workdays. My front neck muscles were stretched and sore from having been snapped backwards. But the three of us had made enough money to repair the car. Our classy '55 Chevy would rise again. I was hooked on the wacky world of demolition derby driving.

My wrecking crew and I raced the Chevy in a mid August demolition derby in Alton, Iowa, but an early September event at Hospers was the last time we were able to drive the '55. It had served its purpose. However, the Hospers event caused me to start experimenting with a driving strategy that would prove effective.

We sought another 25-to-30-dollar junker, eventually locating a prime candidate on George Roseland's farm. George sold us his '58 Ford, which we began preparing for the Sanborn derby in mid September. Demolition derby's popularity had grown rapidly, and forty-three other cars were entered. Another sign of growing interest was when 2,500 spectators filled the stands on the Ed Donkersloot farm on the Thursday night of the big event. Pre-derby advertising had paid off.

I was listening to KIWA Radio Station, quite by accident, when the broadcaster interviewed Gary Ballou, a Northwest Iowa Demolition Derby Association promoter. Ballou related the names of well-known drivers entered at Sanborn. "Loren Flaugh of Archer, one of the better derby drivers, will be in the race," Ballou said.

Hearing my name on the radio felt great, but to know that I had acquired a reputation felt swell. Was this my fifteen minutes of fame?

My car, #44, was entered in the third heat, along with two veteran Sheldon drivers, Ben Dreesen and Roger Jager. These two were good, especially Dreesen. But by now I'd gained enough experience to devise a strategy. Instead of backing away from the starting line to get repositioned, I delayed a second or two. As those in front of me cleared away, I bolted forward into any open spot. In nothing flat I was properly positioned at the perimeter, looking for a victim, while my competition still jockeyed for position.

Dreesen's flamingo-pink Cadillac was my immediate target. I barreled into the Caddy hard as he fought to get his lumbering car into position. The other drivers let Dreesen and me tangle as this became the classic David versus Goliath contest. Though bashing his armored car felt like I was hitting a 70-ton, M-1 Abrams tank, I successfully knocked Dreesen out after several punishing blows. However, the back of my car was now bent up at an acute angle. In short, my car looked like a VW Bug.

The ecstatic throng went wild at the comical sight of #44, for the car was at least two feet shorter, a subcompact sedan, you might say. After Ben and I squared off, only Jager still moved. A couple of punishing blows and he, too, was gone.

The last big collision caused a severe problem. I was declared the winner, but when I left the arena I was actually dragging the fuel tank along on the ground behind me by the teeny-tiny fuel line. Though my car was a sorry sight, I still had a great deal of mobility.

My pit crew went to work at a feverish pace on the fuel tank problem. Since we couldn't see any logical place to reattach it, someone suggested, "Let's put the tank in the back seat, cut a hole through the floor and then run the fuel line through the hole. Nobody can get at the fuel tank back there."

In theory, this seemed to be the best solution. Everyone concurred.

When I drove my car out for the championship heat along with seven other drivers, the crowd buzzed like bees with excitement. How long would Flaugh last? I didn't have high hopes for myself, and perhaps the crowd didn't either. Well, I stunned us all. Only one other car still moved when my #44 finally gave up the ghost.

For a while my crew and I thought we had second place in the bag. But as the judges inspected my car, they quickly discovered the fuel tank in the back seat.

"You guys are disqualified because you've violated a critical safety rule. The fuel tank in the back seat is a serious fire hazard," a judge explained. Our #44 and another car were disqualified.

In conclusion, I couldn't possibly have had more pure fun knocking Dreesen out early. Even the crowd got their money's worth, watching our epic encounter.

There was just one more race in Sheldon later that fall, and then the season ended. I had the next nine months to dream of all the fun I'd have during the 1970 demolition derby season.

Well, I did drive in one race that next summer. But even if I had won that race, it wouldn't have mattered. Demolition driving had lost its luster and wasn't near as much fun as during that endless summer of 1969.

In essence, I think I'd matured during the previous twelve months and started to take life more seriously. With a career in the oil and gas industry emerging, and romance in the air, life took on a greater meaning.

Loren Gaylord Flaugh is someone who has found it easy to master different skills in several work domains, yet mastering the craft of writing remains as elusive as ever.

WHY WOULD ANYONE WANT TO LIVE IN ILLINOIS?

Joanne Campe

"Why would anyone want to live in the state of Illinois?" I asked myself as my parents and I traveled from our summer vacation in Wisconsin, back to Kankakee, Illinois, our hometown. Wisconsin was beautiful. Luscious green hills and valleys, winding roads, beautiful blue lakes and picturesque farms dotted the countryside, with milk cows in the fields.

As we entered Illinois, the land was flat for miles and miles . . . no beauty at all. Corn and beans and wheat and dullness were all I saw. Of course, I was just fifteen years old at the time, and before this vacation had not been out of our state.

Since then, many things have changed. I started dating a guy in high school. He was a farmer. I knew I'd never marry a farmer, especially him—not if he were the last man in the world. I went out with him only so my girlfriend could go out with his friend.

The farmer and I have been married for nearly fifty years.

During our first ten years of married life we lived in the city. My husband had an office job that he seemed to like. We had three children, a nice house, and a car. I thought he was happy, but he kept talking about going back home.

Then his father asked him to come back and help with the farming. Why is it so hard to take the farm out of the farmer? So we moved, and that's where we've been for the past forty years. I learned to be a farm wife—and to appreciate the state of Illinois.

At first my job was in the house, taking care of our small children. Then, when the youngest started kindergarden, I started working in the field.

Oh my, what an experience that was! I learned to drive a tractor and to work the ground. There's nothing like the smell of rich black dirt being worked up. Imagine, me getting turned on by dirt.

And we had pigs, mostly feeder pigs that were bought for market. I fed them when my husband couldn't, and taking food out to a barn full of growing pigs is no fun. I was often lucky to get out of there alive. When they were bigger, and had been moved outside, one of the pigs got out of the pen. I didn't know what to do, so I roped him and tied him to the fence. When my husband saw this he thought he was the laughingstock of the men in the area. He asked me, "How did you get a rope around his neck?"

Wonders never cease on the farm.

One day I was disking a field next to where my husband was plowing. I was on an open tractor and enjoying myself immensely. It felt great to be out of the house and away from the housework. Then my husband came barreling over to the field I was in to ask, "What are you doing?"

"Disking," I replied.

"You don't even have the disks in the ground!" he shouted.

That was just one of the times I quit. I always went back.

In spite of the trials I had learning to be a farmer's wife, I grew to love the wide, open spaces. I could walk out on the porch at night and see the entire sky with its bright, shining moon and twinkly stars. I could even see airplanes taking off from O'Hare Airport. They were far in the distance, as we were ninety miles from Chicago. I thought of them as cars, flying with their lights on.

In the spring, after planting, I would see the corn beginning to sprout in the fields.

Beautiful. It reminded me of a rich, black quilt with little green tufts embroidered on the top. I never grew tired of looking at the fields in our area.

I also loved the smell of fresh-cut hay. The sweet, clean smell was unbeatable on a summer's day, as was the rain as it came across a field, and my being able to watch it as the front moved in closer.

I'll never forget the wonders of living on a farm. We're retired now, and I still have my fond memories. I dread the thought of someday perhaps having to move from here if our house and five acres become too much work for us.

I'm so glad to have learned that Illinois is a beautiful state, with riches beyond compare.

Joanne Campe is a wife, mother, grandmother and great-grandmother. She and her husband farmed in the Herscher, Illinois area for nearly fifty years. She has been published in *The Christian Communicator* and *Message of the Open Bible*.

ELEVATORS

Terry Davenport

I was thirty-two years old and he was even younger. We were just beginning to feel some of the success his years in the Air Force and at the University of Nebraska had earned him. I was a displaced West Virginia girl and had proudly helped out by working in a doctor's office while I also took care of our three children.

His new job had brought us here to my first farm country experience. I was equating the move to having a new home. To making friends we would know for a lifetime. To putting down roots after so many years of moving and planning and saving.

Our first new home was designed, contracted and the footers were just being poured that afternoon. The lot we had purchased was next to the fourth hole of a beautiful golf course near the City Beautiful, Storm Lake, Iowa. It was late summer and I had a worry in my heart that winter would overtake us before the house was finished. We were moving the children to a new school—again—and it was important that they begin this year on the first day of school. They would be less likely then to feel like they were the "newbies."

Our older children, a girl who would enter high school that year, and a boy in ninth grade, were sad about leaving their friends behind. Saying "sad" was putting it politely. There had been crying bouts from the girl, and long periods of silence from the boy. Our youngest son, a second grader, was okay with what was happening. He'd been too young to remember our last move. And, being the youngest, he was used to adversity anyway.

As I watched the concrete slowly slide down the chute and fill the shape I already had stamped on my brain, I heard the hum of an electric golf cart as it came up behind me. I turned to see two smiling women golfers. They introduced themselves to me and pointed out their homes nearby. I told them how many rooms would be in our home, about our children, our cats and dog.

That's when they rocked my world.

"Your children will like the Alta schools," they informed me.

"Alta!" I probably screamed. "Our children are going to Storm Lake to school." And by the way, "Where *is* Alta?"

Fifteen minutes and two miles later, I was sitting in my car across the road from the three gigantic elevators that were Alta to me that day. Just their height made me feel dizzy. So did the questions swirling around in my head.

Do they have a Methodist church here?

What will our two teenagers have to say?

I thought about driving through town to see the schools, but which direction would I go? And what exactly were elevators, anyway?

My new friends had told me about the out-of-district tuition, which was too much for us to even consider, what with the cost of the new house. It was too late to put the concrete back in the mixer. So, Alta it would be.

My tears finally stopped and I made the drive to Storm Lake to break the news to my husband. Things always sounded better to the kids coming from him. Maybe it would sound better to me, too.

Now, I reminisce at sixty-six years of age. We built the house and our two older children graduated from Alta High School. They spent fewer hours on the highway driving to and from school events since Alta was so much closer to our home. For that same reason, it was easier for friends to stop by.

The boys' track meets were announced over the loud speaker system we donated to the school. Our sons were on the football team together, one as a receiver and the other as a ball boy. They both played and marched in the band, though a few years apart.

Our daughter had a wonderful art teacher who nominated her for "Young Iowa Artist of the Year," and that win was the highlight of her senior year. She had her wedding in the new church we helped build.

Looking back over the years, our children would have made their way no matter where we had lived, but we all love having made a life in a smaller town. We each still have friends here that we cherish. Friends from school. Friends from the PTA. Friends from church. From an excellent public library squeezed into a tiny storefront, where I made friends with the volunteer librarian who loved books and was wonderful to talk with about whatever we were reading at the time.

We experienced productions by the local theater and enjoyed them more than maybe the talent merited, just because we knew everyone in the cast.

I made my first "pan of bars" for a PTA bake sale. I knew pies, but "bars"?

So many priceless memories of those years.

Best of all, for me, I still love it when those elevators are full and we get to see that big, beautiful mountain of golden grain temporarily piled upon a flat space at the county fairgrounds . . . just about the time school starts each year in Alta.

Terry Davenport is the grandmother of three girls and three boys and still lives in Buena Vista County, Iowa. Happily, after thirty-plus years, she understands the country and loves living there.

Photograph by Dan Ruf

THE LOFT

Dan Ruf

The hayloft lies quiet now. Amid the whistling wind and scattering of broken bales of hay a few pigeons can be heard cooing in the rafters. The swallows are busy mudding in their new nests for the next generation of young, but other than these winged inhabitants and a few mice scurrying about, this loft's past is a secret to all but the aging minds of those who worked and played inside this rural cathedral.

Years ago, when the importance of the loft was second only to the farmhouse that stood in view of this storage facility, it was not only a place where bales of straw or hay were sheltered from the outside elements, it was a workplace, a school and a playground for the boys and girls of the rural community.

Several times during the year farmers and their sons and daughters came together at this loft to put up the year's supply of hay or straw for the livestock that the loft also sheltered. Tractors and conveyors were rolled into place, waiting for the hayracks that would soon be pulled into place to be off-loaded of their bales. While the men and boys loaded, unloaded and stacked the loft's contents the women usually would be busy preparing the noon meal to feed the hungry workforce. In the barn, sons were being taught at an early age the proper techniques for stacking the bales so that the walls of bales were straight, secure and tight.

The importance of the loft as a school came into play while the young men and boys stood next to fathers and grandfathers during the working process. The importance of hard work, fair play and group effort for a common cause were molded into their consciousness amid the recounting of stories and tales of the rural community in which they were from. Young boys felt the pride of working alongside their fathers and other men from the community, each coming of age and gaining a feeling of importance as their place in the farming workplace became secure. Each year their stature in the labor force became more important as they moved from stacking bales in the loft to unloading bales from the hay rack, to driving tractor, to stacking bales from the bailer out in the field. It was during these harvest times that the lessons and work ethic of the family farm became imbedded in them for use when they finished schooling and became members of America's workforce.

In most lofts the remnants of the lighter times of a child's life can still be found. The basketball rim, now sadly dangling from the wall, bears the scars of thousands of jump shots and dunks by the long ago youths that played here. It watched as the youngster concentrated on sinking the final foul shot that would win the imaginary "big game." It was witness to the whispering play-by-play as young hands sought to hone their skills for the day when they could be stars on Friday nights in town gyms.

On the wall of this old loft was the commonly painted circle or "bulls eye" that became the target for the young arm learning to pitch for the first time. As time went by, the ball was thrown straighter and truer and with growing pride. The circle is alone now. Faded and worn from the constant impact of the leathered surface which sought its heart. It has watched as countless youngsters "leaned in," looking for the sign for the next pitch. It has heard the cry of the crowd from the young voice as the white, scuffed ball found its home for the game-breaking pitch. But all is quiet now.

Young girls played up here or sought refuge to dwell on life's looming questions about maturing into young women. Many a diary was stored here, hidden from the prying hands and eyes of younger sisters and brothers, and filled daily with the events and musings of a growing mind. As the girls grew into womanhood, counseling sessions took place with close friends about growing up, the maturing young souls and young men. No matter what the subject, the times spent in the loft were invaluable to their future station in life as women, wives and mothers.

So this loft, this giant, empty edifice, was one of the most important housings in this farmyard. It stood through countless seasons, being filled and emptied of its cargo, to supply the foodstuffs or bedding for the livestock that fed and helped rear these farm families. It watched as children grew into young men and women, and listened in silence to their changing lives. It watched as the sons and daughters left home for new lives and even saw them return years later with their own children. A whole new generation then put this loft to use much the same way as their fathers and mothers had in years past.

This sanctuary, this sanctuary of life's lessons is idle now. Home to few living things, but the keeper of volumes of memories of days gone by. And soon it will disappear from this earth. The only evidence of its existence will be found in the minds of those that found its warm protective walls a haven during their lives. But in the not too distant future, no evidence will exist of this place. For the people whose memories recounted the stories of this place will be gone, and the children who heard these stories will be gone.

But I stand here, on this hallowed ground, with my

camera, remembering my years in the loft. I can smell the fresh hay as it waits for the next feeding. It reminds me of the summer when it was taken. I can feel the warmth of that summer in my consciousness. I can hear the steady rumbling of the hay conveyor as it delivered a steady stream of green bales. I can also see my sons working. Even though they are gone far from this farm, I feel their presence near me. I can see the beads of sweat running down the sides of their faces. I see my daughter playing with the countless kittens that used this barn as a safe haven. I hear the laughter of my children as they swung on the rope that hung from the rafters.

This is the final generation for this loft. The stories of farm life rest with these children, for the loft is gone now and the children are gone, as well. Gone to new lives and relationships, far from the sounds and smells of this loft. But it is in them, it is in their souls.

Dan Ruf is a retired Northwest Iowa farmer, serving his other two passions of photography and writing from his home in Spirit Lake, Iowa.

FOUR HOURS IN THE WELL

Grace Hoffman

When I was five years old I fell down a well on our farm property and became, for a short time, something of a local celebrity. The story "When Gracie Fell in the Well," as it came to be known over the years, has been repeated hundreds of times, no doubt, but all I have to show for the harrowing experience is a scar on my left knee.

My sister Janice was supposed to be watching me. Janice was ten, and she didn't like it when she had to act as babysitter.

"I don't want her tagging along," she complained on that Saturday afternoon after our mother had told her she'd have to keep me with her. "I'm going over to Dee's house. We're going to paint. She got a new watercolor set for her birthday."

"Well, Gracie would probably enjoy doing that," Mom said. She was at the sink, her hands soapy from washing the dinner dishes, and she turned to look at us. Her expression clearly said, *don't argue with me*, but Janice was never one to leave well enough alone.

"She's too little. She'll spoil everything!" Janice insisted.

Mom put a hand on one hip. Considering it was still covered with soapsuds, even I recognized this gesture as an indication of serious irritation. Janice wisely realized that arguing would be a mistake. "C'mon," she said to me through gritted teeth, and took my hand. Mom turned back

135

to her dishes and Janice pulled me roughly toward the door. "You can hang around with us, but you better not get in the way," she added.

"I want to paint, too," I said as we reached the kitchen door.

"Forget it," Janice mumbled under her breath.

"Mom!"

Without turning around, Mom said, "Let her paint, Janice."

My triumph was short-lived. Janice nearly pulled my arm from the socket as we left the house. We hurried across the yard, to the field that separated our property from the next farm, where Janice's best friend Dee lived. We'd crossed that field many times, and we thought we knew every inch of it. But there was a strip of land that ran across the north end of the field that we usually shied away from. A mean mule named Rex lived in a pasture on the other side of that fence. Rex had a long neck that he would stretch across the barbed-wire fence to reach anyone within snapping distance of his big, yellow teeth. We'd both been schooled to stay far away from Rex, and that was one rule we always obeyed.

But that day was different. We were halfway across the field when I looked over at Rex's pasture and noticed something new. Rex was there, all right. But he was lying on his side, his feet sticking straight out like a toy that had fallen on its side.

"Hey, look," I said, digging in my heels and bringing Janice to an abrupt halt. "Rex knows a trick."

Janice looked over to where I pointed. Her eyes opened wide and her mouth formed a perfect O. "Rex is dead," she said when she found her voice. She lost track of her irritation with me as our mutual curiosity took over. "That's the rendering truck come to get him."

And there was, in fact, a truck busy backing up to the spot where Rex lay. The truck had a winch on the back with a hook, like the ones we saw that occasionally pulled broken-down cars. We could only imagine what that hook was about to do in relation to poor old Rex. A man hopped out of the truck, and another one came around from the other side. They walked toward Rex.

Janice looked down at me. "Let's get out of here," she said. "Dee's waiting for us." She took my hand, but her tugging was less rough than it had been earlier.

Of course I would have nothing of it. "No!" I yanked my hand free. "I want to watch."

"There's nothing to watch," she said, reaching for me again.

Turning on my heel, I took off. I ran, out of pure orneriness, along the fence line. I felt Janice in hot pursuit but didn't dare stop to see how close she was getting to me. I veered away from the fence, toward the open field. This was new territory to us, a section of the land we'd never crossed before as it was still too close to the neighbor's pasture.

I didn't see the boards in time. The field was overgrown with wild grass and weeds. I didn't see the rotted planks that covered a long-abandoned well until they gave out from under my weight and I crashed through.

The next thing I knew, I was lying doubled-up on my back, in several inches of cold, filthy water, staring up at a tiny patch of blue overhead. My legs were pushed up so my knees were pointing toward my nose. Both knees were scraped, and one held a long cut that bled freely. Disoriented, I had no idea what had just happened or even where I was.

From somewhere far away I heard Janice calling my name. There was an edge of panic in her voice, clear even from this distance.

Slowly, the reality of my situation began to dawn on me. I realized I must have fallen down an old well. I started crying, aware now of not only the iciness of the water that crept up the back of my shirt, but the various scrapes, bumps and bruises I'd incurred on my way down. My back hurt the most, though no worse than when I'd fallen off my bike the week before.

I pulled my legs up and maneuvered around so I was on my hands and knees. I could hear Janice still calling for me, though it seemed she was getting farther away.

"Help!" I yelled. "I fell down! Mommy!" I hadn't called our mother Mommy in ages, but at that moment my mommy was exactly what I wanted. Even though I'd yelled as loudly as I could, my words felt muffled, seeming to bounce back at me.

I was sure no one had heard me.

Getting to my feet, I jumped as high as I could. "I'm here!" I hollered at the top of my lungs.

Now it sounded as though more people were calling for me, searching. Janice must not have seen me fall through the boards. No one knew where I was. With growing desperation, I continued to call out. Fear made my voice high and squeaky, and my words seemed to float around me. Janice's voice grew more distant, so I could barely hear her or the other searchers. That they were hunting for me gave me hope, but as the voices faded to nothingness my hope dissolved and I began to wail in earnest, certain now that I was going to die in the bottom of this well.

I cried out for my mommy and daddy, my hamster Gladys and even Topper, the one-eyed Teddy bear that had been with me since birth but that I'd mostly ignored for the past year. At that moment I would have given just about anything for the comfort of Topper's worn hide.

I yelled until my throat hurt, until I was so weary that I could no longer stand, and I sat in the dirty water.

Exhausted, I must have dozed, my forehead resting on my scraped knees, because when I looked up again the blue patch had grown dull, the scant light dimmer. I no longer heard voices calling my name.

They'd given up. I was sure of it. They had looked long enough, and had probably all gone home for supper. I cried fresh tears, feeling abandoned. I pictured Janice sitting at the kitchen table with Mom and Dad, the three of them probably eating my favorite meal—spaghetti and meatballs—talking about how much they would miss me. Sure, that's what they'd say, but I suspected Janice was secretly happy. And my mother, I was sure, was already planning to turn my bedroom into the sewing room she'd always wanted.

My breath came in hiccuppy little sobs as I imagined how quickly they would forget me. Janice had told me several times that she'd wanted a little brother and had been disappointed when I'd come along. Maybe I *hadn't* fallen through those boards on my own. Maybe Janice had—

"Here she is!"

Jerked out of my fantasies, I looked up and saw Janice's very small face blocking out a portion of the blue above.

"Jannie!" I cried, and this time my voice did carry, as was evident by the joy on my sister's face.

"She's down here!" Janice yelled at someone behind her. "She's okay!" She looked down at me again. "*Are* you okay?" she called to me.

"I-I th-think so," I sobbed.

Then Janice was gone, and another face appeared in her place. Our father's. Then Mom's, right beside him. They crowded against each other, each trying to look down at me.

"Oh, baby," Mom wept. "We're going to get you out of there."

At the sight of my parents I blubbered like a two-year-old. "I wanna go home!" I wailed. "I wanna go home *now*!"

"We're going to bring you up," my father said. "Hang tight." They both vanished from sight.

"Don't go!" I shrieked.

Mom's face appeared again. "Gracie, we're going to lower you a rope," she told me. I could hear the tremble in her voice. "When it gets down there, grab onto it and we'll pull you up."

I heard my father talking to someone else. It sounded like there were several people up there, all determined to bring me to safety.

As my mother had promised, a rope snaked down the side of the well, dangling in front of my nose before I was able to grab onto the knotted end of it. But as they tried to lift me, I lost my grip on the knot and fell back into the water with a splash. I cried again, scared, but also furious at my predicament. It wasn't fair!

Janice appeared in the opening above. "You can do it," she yelled down at me. "Pretend it's the rope we swing across the creek on." When somebody next to her spoke, she turned and said, "Just sometimes."

The rope came down again, but again I couldn't hold onto it. There was talk of a ladder, but I was too far down for a ladder to reach. I caught glimpses of more faces. The patch of blue faded and shadows lengthened. Lights were set up, and they glared down white into the well, so it was hard for me to look up.

After what seemed a long time, my father said, "We're going to try something else, Gracie."

There was much clattering and banging. Then something was being lowered slowly down to me. I recognized the hook that had been attached to the winch on the back of the rendering truck. The same hook that the men had been preparing to use on poor old Rex.

It worked. The hook was big enough that I was able to sit on it. When I yelled that I was ready, there was the rumbling of an engine and I was slowly lifted up, out of the well. As soon as I reached the rim my father grabbed me and pulled me the rest of the way out, and set me firmly on the ground. My mother threw her arms around me and hugged me tighter than she ever had.

There were at least a dozen people standing around, and someone took a picture with a flash camera. They patted my father on the back, offering their congratulations on my safe return. Even Janice hugged me when she got the chance.

The next day the whole town was talking about my experience. We went to church, as we always did on Sundays, and it seemed that everyone turned in the pews to look at us. I felt very important. My picture even appeared on the front page of our small local newspaper.

After a while, the excitement died down and things returned to normal. Even Janice, who was especially nice to me for a few days, went back to her old self.

The old well was filled in and more securely sealed, and Rex had long since been hauled away. Janice went back to resenting having to watch me. But she was never again quite as mean to me as she had been before my four hours in the well.

Grace Gerard Hoffman grew up on her family's farm in Minnesota, which was lost to the auctioneers during the farm crisis of the 1980s. She's an artist and illustrator, now living in Texas.

WALKING BEANS WASN'T SOMETHING YOU DID WITH YOUR DOG

MY FIRST JOB

Sharon Parriott

Frankly, I think my sister was jealous.

She was older by twenty-one months. I remember that number because when anyone asked Mom, she always said, "The girls are twenty-one months apart." I always found that curious, but I suppose it was not one and a half years, nor was it two years; she seemed to want to express it exactly.

My sister was jealous of my first job because she didn't think of it first and I insisted that I do it alone. And I did receive family acclaim, my level of esteem raised considerably.

I was the youngest of four children in a farm family, and somewhat of a favorite. At least that's what my sister would say. So when I made my offer, she felt upstaged. I was firm that I wished to do this individually and wanted no assistance from my mother or sister . . . nyeh . . . nyeh.

Breakfast was my favorite meal. The freshness, the serenity of a summer morning that started out cool and quiet and progressed in a predictable way toward the daily farm activities had a reassuring rhythm. Each morning seemed problem-free, offering a new beginning.

It was the summer I was entering sixth grade that I made this offer to my mother: "I want you to sleep in every morning and I will be in charge of breakfast. I want to cook it and serve it to the men when they come in from the chores, and then to you when you get up."

My mother thought a moment. "Well, you know, they bring up the milk can from the barn and that cream has to be separated and cooled right away."

"I know," I answered. "I've done that for you anyway. I can do that while they eat." The big soup ladle was the instrument for the skimming and I knew how to use it.

She smiled and, as always, I felt her confidence in me.

Are there any menus tastier than those served at 6:00 a.m. on a cool summer morning? There's fresh dew on the grass, birds chirping their merry messages and the screen door is free of the feisty flies that would plaster it by afternoon.

I didn't have to ask the morning crew, "What would you like for breakfast?"

I chopped up the potatoes with the cut edge of a tin can that had been punctured with air holes. I fried the bacon and sausage, scrambled eggs, brewed the coffee, poured the orange juice and milk. Some mornings I fixed pancakes or French toast.

My two teen brothers requested cornbread some mornings. This was called Johnnycake, and Mom added bran to firm it up. It was delicious with honey or syrup. One hired man thought this was a real delicacy.

I grew up a lot that summer. I think it was my first taste of male adoration.

My sister aged a bit, too, and found me less submissive to her many directions.

Breakfast is still my favorite meal.

Sharon Parriott lives in the Okoboji, Iowa area. She has enjoyed teaching and writers' groups for twenty years, and writes in many different genres. She is a patron for all the arts always encouraging others to participate.

THE LITTLE BOY WHO LOVED ME

Shirley Roberts

The year was 1950 and I was thirteen years old. My parents faced a dilemma. I, their youngest child, had graduated from eighth grade country school, and it was time for me to move on to high school. Driving the ten miles to the school every day was out of the question due to the dirt roads and the deep snow that fell regularly during the winter months in Nebraska.

In the past, my siblings had lived with family members near the school, or rented a room in town. But nothing was available for me in or near our small town.

My father was sixty years old, and maintaining the huge farm by himself was an overwhelming task with no children other than myself left at home to help. My parents decided the solution was to downsize, and they purchased a smaller farm just two miles from the high school.

Thus I began my freshman year of high school, trudging the long route to and from school every day. I didn't mind or complain, as it was a great solution to the problem. And, after all, our "new" house had electricity and running water, something that had been unavailable in our remote farmhouse.

On my way to high school every day I walked past another farm, where eight-year-old Bryce lived. I watched for Bryce, and we would walk together every morning, and after school as well. He was very quiet, shy and polite. I would ply him with questions about school and sports in an effort to get him to talk.

When Bryce placed second in the county spelling bee he shared his disappointment with me the next morning.

"Hey, you shouldn't be disappointed," I said. "That's a big deal. You should feel very proud."

In my senior year of high school, I was candidate for homecoming queen. After the results had been announced, we walked home together.

"Did you win?" he asked, excitedly.

I was surprised at his interest. "No," I said.

He hung his head. "I would have voted for you, if I were old enough."

I smiled at him and responded gently, "I know. But don't be disappointed. I was elected editor of the year book."

He was not impressed.

Although we walked many miles together, I don't really remember making any special effort to be that little boy's friend—being nice to him just seemed like the right thing to do. Many years later I learned an important lesson about those walks with Bryce.

Each grade in my high school consisted of fifteen to twenty-five students, and didn't change much over the years. It was decided to hold an "All High School Reunion" every five years. The first weekend in August was chosen as a permanent date, and everyone associated with the school was invited to attend. Even now, decades later, hundreds of people of all ages plan their trips back to that small town in Nebraska every five years.

On the Saturday night of the reunion we have dinner with our classmates. On Sunday morning a church service is held in the park, followed by a catered meal. People spend the day mingling with their classmates, as well as their classmates' parents, siblings, spouses and children. It's a delightful event.

At the reunion in August of 2000, a handsome, gray-haired man walked up to me. I immediately recognized the name on his nametag. This gentleman was Bryce, my former neighbor. Bryce and I greeted each other warmly, and after a few minutes of conversation he said, "I bet you didn't know I was madly in love with you when you were in high school."

I giggled. Of course I had no idea!

He proceeded to explain. "You always watched for me and we'd walk to school together. You were always so nice and sweet. Not only did I love you, but also I hated the guys who flirted with you. I can remember being in town with my dad, and I would see you riding around with your boyfriend, Larry. You were always with Larry and I hated him more than any of the other guys."

We enjoyed laughing over the infatuation that eight year old boy had over an "older woman"—me.

In August 2005, Bryce and I met again at the reunion picnic and stopped to visit. My niece, who knew the story, walked past as we were chatting and asked to take our photograph. I sat on Bryce's lap, and we laughed as I put my arm around his shoulder. That photo is priceless to me.

I tell this story to family and friends because it's been an important lesson to me. We don't know when a small kindness will touch another person.

In fact we may never know—or it may take fifty years before someone steps forward to say, "I want you to know how special you were ..."

Shirley Roberts is retired and living in Cincinnati, Ohio. She enjoys writing stories for her six grandchildren and hopes to motivate and inspire them by sharing her experiences.

Photo provided by Robin Munson

WILDFLOWERS

Robin Munson

Gazing out the window of our 1979 Chevy wagon, I realized the moment I had been waiting for all year was here. Like the past eight years, the prolonged anticipation was jerked into reality by the dawning of the last Saturday in June.

"Hey, quit daydreaming and get under here!" yelled my sister. My window already down, I joined my sister and two brothers sandwiched between two open sleeping bags.

"Dad, roll down the window please," sang a chorus of voices. He tilted his head, crowned with his lucky fishing hat, smiled in the rear view mirror, and pushed the button to release the window.

Whoosh! The wind came in with a vengeance and attacked the top sleeping bag. The four of us held tight to the sides until it was secured into any available crack or crevice. We lay down laughing at the parachute above. It was a wonderful way to stay cool without the comfort of air conditioning.

I sat mesmerized by the flapping of the tarp corners bungeed to the trailer in tow. The trailer was packed with enough clothes, food, and bug spray for a family of six to survive a weeklong vacation at Balm Lake in Northern Minnesota. The cabin was a place for our family to escape the suburban niceties and to let loose in the country. As I sat underneath our homemade parachute, I reminisced about the past eight years at Balm Lake and noted the contrast between my short time in the country versus living in the suburbs.

Before every trip my mom spent time going down every aisle of our suburban supermarket, picking just the right food for the mini-kitchen in the cabin. She expanded the kitchen by using an electric griddle to whip up a batch of French toast, a treat we only had at the cabin.

One year we gorged ourselves on French toast, diminishing our bread supply to a few crumbs. I accompanied my dad to the nearest town to buy more bread. The closest town to Balm Lake was Debs. The whole town consisted of the Debs General Store, and nothing else.

"You can smell cat in that place the moment you open the door," my mom often said.

Yes, it was true. Debs's one-room general store had an abundance of cats and a shortage of litter boxes. Our mom avoided the store whenever possible. For someone used to the clean crispness of the suburban supermarkets, the dark, musty store where you could buy food, along with bait and tackle, was less than desirable. To the people of Debs, and the surrounding community, the General Store was a place to reminisce about the past, chat about the day's catch and dream about the one that got away. The General Store was the core of the community, filled with everything they needed.

In the suburbs the chemically enhanced lawns were always nicely mowed. I recall waiting for the bus with my feet poised on the edge of the grass. Pleasing my mother by not being on the road and, at the same time, trying not to irritate the neighbor, whose lawn the bus stop was on. He let me wait for the bus on his lawn through kindergarten. Then he called the school and explained to them how my shoe imprints disrupted the uniformity of his lawn. After that the school district moved the bus stop a few blocks down the road to an intersection wide enough for me to wait on the concrete.

Balm Lake was different. The grass grew tall and the flowers grew wild. We were free to run, romp and roam wherever our bodies took us. Our feet became rough and calloused, while our fingers retained a water-soaked pucker throughout the week. During the days we roamed the woods, picked wild raspberries, caught fireflies and swam.

One summer my sister and I quietly waded into the lake. We stood still until we felt the first feathery tickle of a minnow. And then another. And another, until the whole school of minnows was nibbling at our ankles. As our giggles turned into roars of laughter, we stood firm. The first to run lost the game. I held on, wishing I hadn't just had a full can of grape soda pop. But the water, the soda pop, the tickling was soon too much for me. As my bladder released, I dropped down into the water, feigning a fall.

I lost the game, but kept my secret.

At night we released the day's catch of fireflies in the front porch and watched the light show as we drifted off to sleep.

In the suburbs we lived about five blocks from a large lake. It bustled with motorboats, sailboats, and yachts. From our neighborhood beach, equipped with diving board, high dive and a lifeguard, I watched the parade of boats. People sat on the bows, sterns, or any flat surface drenched in baby oil, praying to the Sun God to deliver them from tan lines. I imagined them sliding off the boats like seals on ice—Plop! Plop! Ker plunk!

Balm Lake, on the other hand, was quiet most of the time. Except for the early morning and late afternoon buzz of our dad's tin fishing boat, we rarely saw or heard another boat. The "beach" consisted of about two feet of sand and a rickety dock. We caught and released pumpkin fish, perch, and sunfish from the dock. And from the dock

I shared a bag of cheese puffs with the fish. I enjoyed watching them fight over every last morsel, and they even nibbled the cheese off my fingertips.

For a while the beach boasted a big metal slide. According to my mom, "You went down so many times you wore a hole in your bikini bottoms." Being only four at the time of the incident, my memory consists of my mom telling that story over and over again.

We brought lots of floating devices to Balm Lake, and each day we took part in the ritual of baptizing the inner tubes. We rolled, threw or bounced the inner tubes into the water, careful all the while not to touch the scorching black rubber. Then splash, flop, splash, flop, splash, flop—until the rubber finally became cool to the touch.

Of course, nature has its downfall. A painful bite from a horsefly could bring tears to anyone's eye.

"They're God's punishment for peeing in the lake," my uncle would say. If that were the case, I certainly deserved my share of bites.

My uncle also told me that snakes lived in the old outhouse behind the cabin. "They'll bite your butt!" he warned.

I was thankful our cabin came equipped with a tiny bath, otherwise it would have been just one more reason to pee in the lake.

Every year, it seemed the quiet lake was disturbed by a terrible storm. The storm of 1977 proved to be particularly fierce. My sister and I moved out of the leaky front porch we normally slept in, to higher ground in the living room.

We got a knock on our door from a drenched neighbor, looking for his missing boat. Our father threw on his rain gear and braved the weather to help. More curious than scared, the four of us kids tiptoed around the pots and pans scattered about the porch floor to look out the window. We spotted our dad intermittently between brief flashes of lightning. His rain parka, blown stiff to the side, providing zero protection. Eventually we saw the bobbing of his flashlight coming closer, and we were all greatly relieved. He entered drenched without having been of help to the man.

We retreated to our sleeping bags in the living room and fell asleep to a pots and pan symphony, directed by my mother.

Back in the station wagon, the sleeping bag falling on top of me interrupted my thoughts. Dad had rolled up the window, disrupting the wind tunnel we'd enjoyed for five hours. The smell of dirt filled my nostrils and I knew we had ten more miles to go.

I watched the dust fly from the dirt road and heard the clanking of rocks in the wheel-well.

We reached the lake, stiff and windblown, but also energized. We had a week to swim, explore, and get dirty. What more could a kid ask for?

At the time I didn't realize this would be our last year at Balm Lake. We spent the week swimming and playing as usual.

On the ride home we sat under our parachute and belted out Juice Newton's "Queen of Hearts." We proudly showed our new scabs and bites.

I'm glad I didn't know we would never return. My last year was not tainted by tears.

But who knows? I have a family now. Maybe we'll be heading up to Northern Minnesota in our minivan, don't cha know?

Robin Munson grew up in Minnetonka, Minnesota. She currently lives with her husband and twin toddlers in Spencer, Iowa, where she writes children's picture books.

THE GRAVEL PIT

Evelyn Van Maar

Four miles outside of the town I grew up in was an old gravel pit that had been converted to a swimming hole. It had a rickety wooden dock that creaked alarmingly if more than a few people tried to stand on it at the same time.

The Pit, as we called it, was tree-lined, and was a popular gathering spot for families, teenagers, and kids who just wanted a break from the heat and monotony of the summer months.

When I was twelve, my parents finally gave in to my wheedling and let me ride my bike out to The Pit, with a couple of friends, to camp out overnight. This was the ultimate adventure as far as my friends and I were concerned.

On a weekday evening my best friends Anna Oostra and Jackie Tuel arrived at my house on their bicycles. They came equipped with sleeping bags and plenty of snacks. I packed my new transistor radio.

My pack was securely tied to the rear of my bike with a length of twine I'd found in the garage. Anna was lucky enough to have a basket on the front of her bike, and she carried Jackie's stuff along with hers.

We were ready to go.

By the time we headed out, it was already getting dark. I lived on the edge of town, and it was gravel roads all the way to The Pit. We met the occasional car on the way. They always pulled over to the side to give us plenty of room. Sometimes they honked a greeting, and we waved back.

By the time we reached The Pit it was full dark. Anna, who was a Girl Scout and always came prepared, had brought a flashlight. She held it while Jackie and I unpacked the bikes, laying out our sleeping bags and supplies on a strip of grass near the coarse sandy beach leading to the water.

"O-o-oh, it's the Midnight Killer," Anna moaned, holding the flashlight under her chin to give her features an eerie glow.

I propped my transistor radio on a rock and found our favorite station. We had the area to ourselves. If this had been a weekend a few swimmers might still have lingered, especially with the heat wave we'd been experiencing. But on this night we were alone. The temperature had topped 98° earlier in the day. Though it had cooled a bit since the sun went down, the heat trapped in the ground still radiated upward.

It was a perfect night for a swim, and we were ready. Stripping down to the swimsuits we wore under our clothing, we were soon racing each other down the beach, to the dock.

I got there first, Anna close behind and Jackie—who'd stopped to carefully place her glasses beside my radio—bringing up the rear. Back at our campsite I could hear the distant, tinny tunes of an exciting new singer named Elvis Presley wailing into the night. The sky overhead was dotted with stars, so brilliant they seemed almost within reach. A quarter moon peeked over the treetops, rising as though to join in on the fun.

My intention was to execute a perfect, graceful dive into the inky green water. But before I had the chance, Anna slammed into me, sending me belly-flopping into the water. I sank beneath the surface, arms outstretched.

The water was cold, refreshing, and wonderful over my heated skin. I opened my eyes. Moonlight filtered down, illuminating the water and weeds in pale shades of green. There were fish and even turtles in The Pit, but at that moment it seemed I was the only living creature in a cool, mossy underworld.

Splash! Splash! Jackie and Anna dove in and appeared underwater beside me. Jackie grabbed my arm and pulled me to the surface, where we all sputtered and gasped.

"What did you do that for?" I asked them, treading water.

"We saved your life!" Anna said indignantly. "You were drowning."

"No I wasn't."

"You didn't come up," Jackie said. "We thought you were in trouble."

I splashed water at them, then we climbed up onto the dock. We lay there on our backs, looking up at the luminous stars, and talked.

Jackie's brother was getting married in two weeks and she was excited about being asked to serve punch at the reception. She already had a new dress, and her mother had promised she would get a home perm for the occasion.

Anna's father was out of work, and she hated the way he moped around the house, drinking too much and finding fault with everything she did.

I told them my exciting news, that my older sister would be coming home in a few days from the boarding school she'd been at for the past few months. I'd missed her terribly, and was still puzzled as to why she'd left so suddenly, without even saying good-bye to me. But she was on her way home, and that was good enough.

As we talked in hushed tones a car pulled up and drove slowly by our makeshift campsite, then turned and left. Teenagers, we speculated, looking for a place to park and discouraged by our presence.

We swam some more, ate soda crackers with cheese, then, well after midnight, crawled into our sleeping bags. We'd left my transistor radio on and the battery was dead. It didn't matter.

In the morning we creaked and groaned as we got up and stretched our stiff muscles. The ants had gotten into our food, but we brushed them off and finished the last of the grapes.

We packed up and rode our bikes home in time for breakfast with our families.

My friends and I continued to swim at The Pit every summer, until we graduated and went our separate ways.

Anna got married and, after a few years and a few children, moved to Texas so her husband could look for work. He drank too much, just as her father had, and when she stopped writing back to me, we lost touch.

Jackie also moved away, to California. When she came back for a visit I hardly recognized her, with her waist-length hair, wire-rimmed glasses and loosely flowing clothes. She talked about going to sit-ins to protest the war in Vietnam, and told me, with a touch of pride, that she'd been arrested several times.

The Pit was modernized, with outbuildings and a new dock installed. A concession stand was built to sell snacks, and lifeguards went on duty.

Parents nowadays wouldn't dream of letting their children stay out alone overnight. The thought of my own children, or now my grandchildren, staying by themselves at that remote gravel pit, horrifies me.

But it was a more innocent time, when my friends and I rode our bikes along the gravel road and swam in the water, unsupervised, at night.

A boy we knew did drown at The Pit, but that happened during the day, with his family picnicking on the beach less than fifty yards away and dozens of other people nearby.

And, after I was married and a mother, a teenage girl disappeared from the area and was never seen again. Maybe that was the turning point. After that, we parents kept our children closer to home, guarding them fearfully.

I drove by The Pit recently, in the evening. I'd just received word of Jackie's death, and it got me thinking about the night we'd stayed there. The grass was well groomed, and buoys bobbed in the water beyond the shiny metal dock. Nothing about it seemed the same. Even the stars overhead didn't seem as bright.

Several postings announced that it was closed after 8:00 p.m., and NO LOITERING and NO OVERNIGHT CAMPING signs had been erected. I got out of my car, looked out at the water and listened for the ghostly remnant of childish laughter. I heard nothing.

A few minutes later a patrol car cruised by, and parked behind my car. The officer asked me what I was doing there. When I could give him no explanation he suggested, not unkindly, that I should leave.

I took his advice. I don't believe I'll go back.

Evelyn Van Maar grew up in a small town on the Nebraska/Iowa border. She is currently working on her memoir.

Drawing by LaVonne Hansen

The Lake at Mo(u)rningtime

Ann Johnson

Aged, used and worn, perishing water
glacial birthed as pristine
covering crags of rock and shifting sands
shallow and profound pockets of depths
now reflecting polished palest orange,
light begins from above the far darkened
tree line, undefined.

Exceptions of diving and surfacing coots,
looking for decaying vegetation for breakfast fare
to fill them with wing power
a resolve carry them south.

Small puffs of fog emerge from the
warmer than air water,
like wisps of perspiration
emitted to balance the body.

Slowly tree branches and
rooftops define more clearly—
testimony of human components
forced upon this once uncrowded
wilderness beauty
aged and obligated.

Ann Johnson is a mental health counselor and enjoys bicycling, golf, boating, fishing, writing, reading and her family. She has two daughters, and lives in Wahpeton, Iowa with her husband, Wayne.

SMALL TOWN GHOSTS

Rebecca Groff

Walking home from school one day, I came upon what appeared to be the remains of a football player. It was hanging from the light post on the corner of Main Street, in front of our town's only dress shop. The helmet showed no face from its interior, the arms and legs drooped in its jersey and pants, and the cleats on the feet dangled aimlessly in the cool September breeze that afternoon. I was six, maybe seven years old at the time, and it terrified me so badly I ran the rest of the way home to tell my mother what I'd seen.

That was the day I learned what the term "hung in effigy" meant. That defeated-looking dummy represented the hopes of our high school football team for a victory over our rival at the homecoming game, scheduled for later that week.

The intention, of course, was to garner community spirit before the big night—not to scare a young child. That possibility probably hadn't occurred to anyone. I remember my sense of relief as my mother explained it to me, although to this child at the time, it seemed a strange thing for adults to do.

At least when I drive by that same corner these days, I can smile at the memory.

Those of us who spent our formative years under the umbrella of small town life belong to a rare fraternity of humanity that shares a sense of community and place that never completely leaves us. At least that's how it is for me.

During my growing up years I knew the names of the people who lived and worked in every house along the streets and in the stores of my hometown. I knew who gave apples at Halloween and who handed out the big candy bars.

I knew who'd raise a fuss if I roller-skated on the sidewalk in front of their house, and who didn't mind if my sister and I played in the deserted chicken coop in their backyard—as long as we let them know we were there.

I knew whose dog would bite, having found that out the hard way, and whose dog wouldn't.

I knew when a funeral procession was scheduled to go past my house by the appearance of the typed, white-card announcements posted on the front door of the post office.

I knew that the large, friendly man named Tar who worked behind the counter at the Post Office would pull his blue plastic, egg-shaped coin purse from his pocket and give me and my sister a nickel when we tagged along with our mother to buy stamps. And Mom would tell him he shouldn't—smiling as she said it. And she always reminded us to say thank-you. And we always did.

But *always* is an unfair, illusionary word. These days the houses of the tree-lined neighborhoods of my younger days contain strangers. Too many vacant buildings, hollow and sad, line the Main Street of my childhood.

It wasn't always like this, and I'm fortunate to have the memories of when it wasn't. In the years following World War II, and before the farm crisis of the eighties, the place of my childhood was a thriving municipality where Saturday nights were an event. Farm families drove to town to shop for groceries, buy work jeans, take in a movie and maybe grab a hamburger at the café while catching up with their townie friends.

The local teenagers dragged Main Street, driving up and down the modest thoroughfare, checking out the scene before they reached the opposite end of the street. This probably took less than a minute and a half to accomplish, and I'm sure a fair amount of gas was consumed over time in that repetitive practice, but it was basically harmless—as long as no rivals from outlying communities showed up. It was an effective way to see who was in town, who was riding with whom, and who *shouldn't* be riding with whom. A type of gossip chain in its own right.

During the summer months, the Chamber of Commerce sponsored a Saturday night drawing for prizes from atop a flatbed trailer that had been hauled to the center of the town's square. *Gunsmoke* was on television in those days, and we kids loved to watch Marshall Dillon take on the bad guys in Dodge City every Saturday night from eight to nine o'clock. It was possible to finish watching the program and then hop on our bikes and hightail it uptown, arriving just in time for the drawing. Our neighbor boy did this many times. I don't think he ever won anything, however. Neither did I.

Santa Claus always came to town on a Saturday before Christmas each year, sitting high on the local fire truck in the town square. We kids, bundled in puffy snowsuits or wool coats, snow boots and mittens that shielded us from the bite of Iowa's winter, swarmed that fire truck in the town square, collecting orange-red mesh stockings filled with hard candies and small toys that Santa and his helpers tossed to us. As I recall, it really was more fun getting the stocking than eating its contents.

At that early age I was more into the good stuff, the likes of which could be found at the infamous penny candy counter of the local dime store less than a block away. A buffalo head nickel or one thin dime could buy pure happiness at Wright's Five & Dime Store. The storefront sported an archetypal green canvas awning, which the apron-clad owner, tobacco pipe clenched between his teeth, rolled into action every morning before the sun rose too high. At the end of the day he'd reverse the routine.

The owner also ran a harness-making/shoe-repair shop at the back of the store, so the smell of leather, shoe polish, and sweet tobacco framed each visit. The low, pleasant rumble of old men exchanging stories in the hazy back room filtered out to where my sister and I pored over the candy counter, tended by the proprietor's wife who also ran the cash register for him.

Topless candy boxes teased and encouraged us with pink Bazooka bubblegum, Firestix red-hot candies, stacked squares of banana-scented taffy, tootsie rolls and jaw-breakers of every color. It was a dentist's worst nightmare and a child's best dream arranged together on one wooden counter.

Next door to Wright's was Christopherson's Drug Store, outfitted with a soda fountain that today's generation can only read about. And though the store had its own delectable candy counter, the one from which we bought Butter Brickle or Hershey bars for a nickel each, it was the soda fountain that catered to a child's wish for something cold, creamy or frozen. My all-time favorite was the "orange malted"—a scoop of vanilla ice cream, covered with thick, tangy orange syrup and topped with heaping spoonfuls of sweet, gritty malted milk powder.

If only I had a dime for every one of those I consumed!

The five-cent peach ice cream cone that appeared for the month of August was nothing to be snubbed, either.

The solitary druggist, a quiet giant with bushy white caterpillars for eyebrows, was also the store owner. He'd work his magic behind a wall at the back of the store while chewing on his signature half-lit stogie. Pungent cigar smoke blended with the scent of Emeraude by Coty on display at the perfume counter. These were underscored by the aged aroma of the store's wood flooring, topped off by the fizzing Coca-Cola, creating a one-of-a-kind, welcoming fusion to anyone who walked through the front doors.

The apothecary jars with their spiral-shaped lids, and the amber bottles of potions and pills that lined the shelves high above the druggist's work area always fascinated me. It seemed that any ailment could be fixed by whatever those bottles contained.

Emergency weekend service was rare in those days. The stores were, by law, closed on Sundays, as was the way of Iowa back then.

But an earache could force a bending of the rules when necessary. One Sunday I woke up with a throbbing ear, and my mother had no choice but to call our druggist at home. He agreed to go to his store later that day. The comforting oil he provided, and which my mother warmed and dribbled into my ear, eventually brought the needed relief.

Fudgesicles, orange push-ups, boxes of Dutch Masters and White Owl cigars, prismatic rhinestone jewelry sets, and, in season, pink and red heart-shaped boxes of Valentine chocolates were but a few of the items available at the corner drug.

At one time, this small burg with a population of less than a thousand supported three corner gas stations, three grocery stores and two hardware stores, each with its own loyal customers. There was one movie theater, complete with chasing marquee that made Main Street dance with light. The adjacent Sweet Shop served the after-movie crowd on the south end of town, while the Sunny Side Café provided from the north end of the street. Dane's Bowling Alley was a source of entertainment and competition, and the local News Office supplied the citizenry with the goings-on around town in its reliable Thursday edition.

There were three taverns—at least. I always held my breath as I walked past their opened doors, to avoid the stale, sour smelling air that escaped.

Parson's Dress Shop, the store on the corner from which the dummy football player once sagged, carried a fancy variety of women's wear and dresses. There was none of this eight-of-the-same-dress-in-different-sizes apparel common today.

The town had one staid brick bank with prison-like teller windows, one dry cleaner and three car dealerships—Chevrolet, Ford and Chrysler ruled the highways in those days. John Deere and International Harvester dealerships provided for the farmers' needs, as did the local grain elevator when the harvests were done. The dehydrating plant spread a halo of warm, sweet drying alfalfa scent over the community during the season.

The public library resided in a maroon brick building that also housed the city's single fire truck, and the city's jail cell was situated in the back of the building.

One dentist, one medical doctor, one osteopath, one chiropractor and one veterinarian covered healthcare needs for the community.

Men got their hair cut at one of two barbershops, each with a red and white spiraling barber's pole out front. The ladies had their hair done at a couple of beauty parlors, as we called them. Lots of teased, sprayed and tightly permed hair walked out of those shops.

My dad owned and operated the town's welding shop, where I stopped in each day on my way home from school, often collecting a nickel to buy a treat before continuing home. After all, the corner drug was just across the street from Dad's shop!

The three churches—Methodist, Presbyterian and Lutheran—covered the community's spiritual needs. A single plumbing business, two lumberyards and a laundromat that stocked crème soda and Hires Root Beer in its pop machine rounded out our industrious, self-supporting little town.

So many of the people and businesses that created these memories are gone. The candy counter was auctioned off long ago, and the building that had once been the drug store now houses a small bar. The big door to my dad's machine shop no longer rises.

The movie theater where I watched Godzilla tear down power lines and lift trains like they were boxes of Cracker Jacks is today little more than a dark, quiet cave used for storage.

That symbolic football man still lingers above his corner in my memory. In spite of the emptiness I encounter as I drive through my old town, I sense the ghosts of the past hovering behind the filmy, quiet store windows, in the dust-caked interiors.

And as long as I'm capable of remembering, none of them will ever abandon me—nor I them.

Rebecca Groff enjoys writing both non-fiction and fiction, and has published in national and regional magazines, short story anthologies and online literary web sites. The mother of two grown daughters, she resides in Cedar Rapids, Iowa with her husband.

Drawing by LaVonne Hansen. Blue Ribbon winner, Clay County Fair 2005.

ORDER FORM

Mail order form to: Shapato Publishing
PO Box 476
Everly, IA 51301

Please rush _____ copies of

Walking Beans Wasn't Something You Did With Your Dog:
Stories of Growing Up in and Around Small Towns in the Midwest

at $14.00

+ .98 each sales tax

S&H per quantity:

$3.00 for 1 – 3 copies

Enclosed is check or money order for:

$_____ Payable to Shapato Publishing.

NAME:

ADDRESS:

Or order safely online at:

www.ShapatoPublishing.com